How

C000218726

This book is dedicated to my parents
and the editor of this book, F. A. Roberts BEd(Hons).

How to
Pass Exams

W. G. Leader

MIM
Principal, London City College

MACDONALD AND EVANS

Macdonald & Evans Ltd
128 Long Acre, London WC2E 9AN

First published 1984
Reprinted 1984
Reprinted 1985

© Macdonald & Evans Ltd 1984

British Library Cataloguing in Publication Data
Leader, W.G.
    How to pass exams.
    1. Examinations——Great Britain—— Study
    guides
    I. Title
    371.3'028'12   LB3060.57

ISBN 0-7121-0823-8

Typeset in 9/10pt Baskerville by
Photobooks (Bristol) Ltd
and printed in Great Britain by
Richard Clay (The Chaucer Press) Ltd.,
Bungay, Suffolk

Preface

The thought of sitting an exam unfortunately still fills most of us with some apprehension. Many students never receive any instructions or guidance as to how to cope with exam pressures and have unwelcome surprises when they receive their results.

However, students need not wait until the last minute to find out how to apply their hard-won knowledge under formal examination conditions. Examination technique can be taught and learned just like most other subjects, and this book has been written to teach the student just how to set about acquiring this invaluable skill. Unlike other longer books devoted to more general aspects of studying during a course this book concentrates on the period leading up to the exam and the exam itself. It explains to students just how they should use the often considerable knowledge they have to answer effectively a variety of questions within the strict time-limits of an exam.

This book, then, is of prime interest to a wide range of students taking the examinations of a large number of institutes and associations, especially in the business studies field. It will also be of considerable benefit to those taking CSEs and GCE "O" and "A" levels and their equivalents, while the advice on case studies, mini-cases and objective tests—increasingly important features of many exams from "A" level to degree—will be valuable to students taking higher level examinations. Although written on the assumption that most students will be attending a college or other education centre, much of the information contained in this book will also be of use to overseas students and those based at home but who have limited access to educational resources and tutorial counselling, such as those following correspondence and home study courses.

The text covers most of the revision and examination methods currently in use as well as putting forward many new and stimulating ideas which have found success within the author's own college. The facts you ought to know before the exam, how to plan your revision, how to study, how to improve your reading skills and your vocabulary, how to present your work, how the examiners set and mark your papers—these are some of the topics covered in this book. The coverage of case studies, mini-cases, reports and objective tests is of particular importance, and a chapter on orals, aurals and practicals is also included as these too cause no little apprehension among examinees. Competition for jobs or places in higher education, domestic and personal problems of various kinds, financial worries—all these add to the strain of taking an exam. Advice is also offered on these fronts where possible, so that the student can recognise and appreciate the importance of these factors and thereby work out a constructive approach towards overcoming them.

Finally, if you think you already know all about exam technique, I advise you to have a quick look at pages 48–51 before you put this book down. You may be persuaded otherwise!

1984 WL

Contents

CONTENTS

CHAPTER I

The Right Frame of Mind

1. Self-confidence. One of the major reasons for students failing examinations is lack of self-confidence. Other factors are also very important—intelligence, ability to work hard, a knowledge of exam and study techniques—but people who lack self-confidence find it difficult to become motivated enough to use these other qualities. They so often accept that others seem to be more competent than they are and resign themselves to inferior positions, never really achieving their full potential.

Before you read further into this book have confidence in your ability to study and enjoy what you are learning, and above all in your ability to pass your exams. After all, someone thinks you are good enough or you would not be on the course! To help you develop this positive approach here are a few tips.

2. Don't panic! It may seem easy enough to say this if you are not actually taking an exam in the near future, but there really is very little point in wasting your time and energy in this way. If you have prepared yourself for the exam in the correct way and have learned all you need to know about your subject then you have as good a chance as anyone of passing *if you remain calm.*

Remember, panic is a very destructive state of mind. At the very last minute it could ruin all those weeks of hard work. At best you will not get the grade you deserve, at worst you will almost certainly fail.

3. You *are* talented! This is a fact that you must accept if you are to believe in yourself and have the self-confidence to do well. Remember, simply by being able to read or hold a conversation with your friends you make even the most sophisticated computer look stupid!

4. Get yourself organised. This may sound tedious but by being organised you will find studying much easier and you will have more time for relaxing and doing other things which you enjoy. Above all you will find that you have more time to think about things and read your set texts instead of constantly having to rummage through a mess to find important notes.

This book was written to provide you with ideas on how to get yourself organised, but in the first place you should clear—and keep cleared!—a table to study on at home and file all your study notes etc. properly. Bear in mind that the *quantity* of work you produce is not as important as the *quality*. Concentrate first on improving your weak areas—do not waste time re-reading topics about which you are confident.

5. Reduce stress. Anxieties over the speed at which you read, how forgetful you seem to be, getting your work in on time, expressing yourself clearly in your essays, all these contribute to creating a condition of stress. Don't let this happen to you. Talk through any problems you have with your tutor, a friend or friends, your welfare officer or even your doctor. There is no shame in having problems and anxieties—we have all had them at some time for one reason or another.

Although there may not seem to be any connection, problems related to stress are often a result of your life-style. You should eat food that gives you plenty of nutrition, and you should get adequate sleep and plenty of exercise. If you do catch a cold or are simply just "under the weather", things will seem to get on top of you easily. If you keep a healthy body you will find it helps you to keep a healthy mind too.

Always remember that, if you do have problems, talking about them with your family, welfare officer or even your friends will help, and it may also help you realise that you are not the only one with similar anxieties!

6. Set yourself objectives. A lot of students mistakenly believe that the sole objective of a course is to pass the final examinations. However, when properly analysed your true objective in taking a particular course is more than likely to be to enrich your life through obtaining a good job or increasing your understanding of the world, yourself and other people. These long-term objectives should help you put your exams into their proper perspective, after all it is not the end of the world if you fail in a few!

7. Conclusion. Finally, it is worth remembering that you have probably already learned a great deal during the year that can be consolidated in the weeks leading up to the exams as you revise. All you really need is to believe in yourself, and with the skills outlined in this book in a short time you will be able to approach any exam with confidence and the expectation of success.

CHECKLIST

1. Have confidence in your own abilities. Do not become discouraged by other people *appearing* to be better than you are.
2. Stay calm! Do not waste your energy or valuable time on pointless anxiety.
3. Organise your time wisely and adjust your life-style to keep yourself fit and healthy.

CHAPTER II

Getting the Facts

"Education makes people easy to lead, but difficult
to drive, easy to govern but impossible to enslave."
Lord Brougham

WHAT YOU NEED TO KNOW

1. The facts. There is no point in preparing for an exam until
you have all the facts about it at your fingertips. You may well be
preparing for completely the wrong exam otherwise! This sounds
absurd but it is true—an alarming number of candidates,
particularly those studying privately, enter for the wrong exam,
turn up on the wrong date, mix up practical with theory and even
fail to register in time to be entered for the exam at all! The
following paragraphs outline the type of information you will
require before you start revising.

2. The examining authority. You should first find out the
name and the address of the examining authority whose
examinations you intend taking. Most students will know the
name and so it will be a simple task to locate their address, but
others may find it a little more difficult. Working through the
following list of possible sources of information should help you.

(a) The careers officer or headmaster in your school or college.
(b) Your local, central or educational library.
(c) Educational bookshops.
(d) If you are taking the exams of an independent examining
authority such as professional exams in law or accountancy a

member of that profession may be able to give you the relevant names and addresses as well as advice on how to proceed further.

(*e*) The educational advisory sections of embassies, high commissions, councils, etc. of the particular country where the examining authority is located.

(*f*) The Department of Education in the country where you intend to study.

Once you have found out the address you can then write regarding your particular course (*see* **4** below), or enquire about past examination papers (*see* **9** below), specimen answers (*see* **10** below), Examiners' Reports (*see* **11** below) and so on. These together with other useful information are generally offered for sale to everyone as a public service so you do not need to be a teacher or a college to obtain copies. Copies of publications lists which set out prices and postage costs are also generally available.

3. The syllabus. Without this you cannot know what you should be revising. Usually the student can rely on the tutor to ensure that he or she is taught the complete syllabus, and yet I have often come across tutors who for one reason or another have failed to do so. You can obtain the syllabus as follows.

(*a*) If you are sitting for the exams of an external examining body, they will often—if asked—send you not only the syllabus but will indicate precisely which topics are more important than others. You must know this in order to allocate your revision time properly.

(*b*) If you will be sitting an internally set and marked exam the complete printed syllabus and a selection of past papers can be obtained from your head of department or tutor. Check with your tutor as well to see if there will be any radical change in approach in the forthcoming exam.

Having obtained the syllabus check it against your lecture notes to see if any major parts of the syllabus have not been taught.

4. Type of assessment-standards. The examining body will also provide details of the type of assessment that they apply. Never assume that because your tutor has given you an average mark of 60 per cent for your class or homework that you will pass an examination whose pass mark is 50 per cent.

If your examining body normally expects about 55 per cent of students to pass its examinations and suddenly 95 per cent of them are classified as passes—possibly due to an easy paper—the examining body would probably check the papers again and adjust the marks accordingly to ensure that its usual standards are maintained. Again, there may have been a significant improvement in the standard of the students for that exam. In this case an average student who would have done well enough to pass previous exams could well fail since only a certain percentage of students can be classified as a pass.

It is also worth bearing in mind the type of examining authority whose exams you will be taking. The pass rates for exams set by professional bodies such as in accountancy and law are much lower than for those set by non-professional or academic bodies.

Remember, all examining bodies are quite rightly concerned with consistently trying to maintain and/or improve their standards, so never aim just to pass the examination. Go for a good pass and allow yourself to feel more confident that you will get through.

5. Requirements for the actual examination. Find out precisely what format the exam will follow. It could be any of the following.

(a) *Written exam.* Does it comprise more than one paper? Are there compulsory topics to be answered from each paper? Is one paper an objective test where only one answer is possible for each question? If it is a maths or physics type of exam can you take a calculator into the examination room?

(b) *Oral exam.* Does it involve listening to a tape, reading some literature, making a short speech or will it simply be a dialogue between examinee and examiner? All these are "oral exams", but each requires different techniques and abilities. You may need to practise with several friends.

(c) *Practical test.* This could simply be a laboratory experiment or it might involve demonstrating a skill such as producing something on a lathe, flying a plane or painting a picture. Can you obtain facilities for plenty of practice revision before the test? Do you have to take any instruments to the examination?

(d) *Continuous assessment.* Here it is very likely that your overall grade will be affected by the coursework you produce during the academic year. If it is, it will be extremely important to take this into account when assessing the mark you must obtain in the exam irrespective of the pass mark for the exam itself.

6. Time allowed in the examination. You should also find out exactly how much time is allocated for answering each part or question. You should then practise completing answers to past papers *within the allocated time* during revision.

"But this says your exams are miles from here at Parliament Hill Fields near Highgate. This is Parliament in Westminster!"

7. Where will the examination be held? Once you know the address make absolutely sure that you know how to get there with at least 30 minutes to spare. It is important that you write the address down and carry it with you. This particularly applies to overseas students who may not be familiar with the town where the exam is to be held.

8. Dates and times of the exam. Make a note of this information and keep it on you in a safe place. Check that you have not confused, for example, a practical exam for a written one or "O" level for "A". Most of us at some time in our lives have turned up for an event at the wrong time or in the wrong place. Don't *assume* everything is OK.

9. Past examination papers. These may be obtained from the examining body, whether internal or external. Check the questions against the topics listed in the syllabus.

If the syllabus does not indicate which topics require more emphasis, get hold of several past papers and see which questions tend to appear most frequently. This will give you an idea as to which topics are the most important to revise. However, be very careful to check that the examining body has not changed (or intends to change) the syllabus or examination format before you begin to revise.

10. Specimen answers. External examination bodies sometimes provide model or specimen answers for previous exams. If this is the case try to get hold of as many as you can. They will give you a good indication of the standard of work required.

11. Examiners' Reports. Many examining bodies assist both students and tutors by publishing Examiners' Reports. These analyse the major errors made in examinees' answers with regard to every question that appeared on the previous examination paper. The Reports provide a great deal of detailed guidance to help you understand what is required from you when you answer examination questions.

Along with the Examiners' Report it is also a good idea to check the failure rates in your particular exam field which are also published by the examining authorities—some are surprisingly high! If nothing else this will probably give you the right incentive to concentrate on your studies and revision, while the Examiners' Report will give you an indication of what to look out for to avoid adding to the fail statistics.

SITTING FOR MORE THAN ONE EXAMINATION

12. Method. Many students now sit more than one examination at roughly the same time. These may be:

(a) for two or more different examining bodies for the same subject or subjects at the same level;

(b) for a different examining body for the same subject or subjects but at a different (usually lower) level;

(c) for a specialist examination whilst sitting examinations for a more general course such as a degree.

Make sure that you fully understand the standard of the second examination, and that you have completely covered the syllabus. If the exams are at the same level but held by different examining bodies check that there is no clash of examination times. Where there is a clash the authorities may allow you to be escorted from one location to the other by a tutor so that you do not communicate with examinees who have just taken the exam you are about to take.

13. Advantages and disadvantages of sitting more than one exam. The advantages of undertaking a second exam are as follows.

(a) You increase your chances of achieving a pass in that subject. If you are only taking one exam it is possible you may be ill, late or off-form on that one occasion.

(b) Students who sit an additional specialised examination subject (e.g. for a professional body) are taking the opportunity to add to their qualifications whilst already geared up for studying on the more general course, rather than waiting until this is completed and trying for the professional exams when time may be less readily available and the inclination absent.

(c) Sometimes students wish to ensure that they obtain a qualification at every step of their education and so sit other exams whilst undertaking a longer course of study. In this way, if they fail to achieve their ultimate qualification, they will at least have achieved some qualification rather than none at all.

There are, of course, disadvantages too. Any good tutor wants his or her students to succeed. They may see possibilities or problems of which you may be unaware. If you intend taking a second examination you would be well advised to discuss the matter with your subject or course tutor before going ahead.

CHECKLIST

1. Obtain the examining body's current syllabus, past papers and a recent Examiners' Report.
2. Check the location and the exact times of the examinations.
3. Obtain any specimen questions and answers from the examining body.
4. Check whether or not it is advisable to sit more than one examination.

CHAPTER III

Planning for Revision

"People don't realise that it takes time and effort and preparation to think."

Bertrand Russell

REVISION PLANS

1. Introduction. Having obtained all the major facts that you need regarding your examination you will find that you can now start to plan your revision with an easier frame of mind.

2. Timetables. Before you start your revision it is important to draw up a timetable. This will help you stay on target with your revision and ensure that the relevant topics and tests are covered before your exam. Before drawing up the table it is worth asking yourself a number of relevant questions—and giving honest answers! For instance:

(*a*) *How much time do I have available?* How much time do you have available each week for extra studies and how long is it to the exams? If there isn't enough time to revise each subject entirely and do the necessary tests then make certain that you allocate enough time at least for the major topics.

(*b*) *What are my priorities?* In which topics are you weakest? If you are weak in a major topic revise that first so that you have time to absorb the information gradually.

(*c*) *Have I completed all my set work?* If you have not completed all the work set by your tutor do so immediately. It will be good revision exercise.

(d) *What sort of person am I?* You should also ask yourself some basic questions about yourself. Do you become irritable if you study too much without a break? Will your health or eating habits suffer if you do not allow yourself enough leisure time?

Once you have answered these sorts of questions you can start designing a timetable to suit your own particular needs. Bear in mind that you will probably be attending revision classes at your college as well, so it is advisable to consult your tutor over your revision plans so that you can integrate your personal plans with

Subjects:
1. History
2. Law
3. Economics
4. Maths
5. English
6. Statistics

	Monday	Tuesday	Wednesday	Thursday	Friday	Saturday	Sunday
9.00	History lecture	← FREE →			Statistics lecture		
10.00	History lecture	English lecture	Revision	Revision	Statistics lecture		
11.00	Law lecture	English lecture	Economics Lecture	Maths lecture	History lecture		
12.00	Law lecture	Revision	Economics lecture	Maths lecture	Revision		
1.00	← LUNCH →					FREE	
2.00	Revision	Maths lecture	Revision	Law lecture	English lecture		
3.00	Economics lecture	Maths lecture	Revision	Statistics lecture	English lecture		
4.00	Revision	Revision	Revision	Revision	Revision		
5.00	Revision	Revision	Revision	Revision	Revision		
6.00	← DINNER →						
7.00	English Revision	Economics Revision	Maths Revision	Statistics Revision	History Revision		
8.00							
9.00							

Additional Information ___32 hours revision time (total)___

FIG. 1. *A revision timetable.*

revision work covered at college or school. Your tutor may also be willing to let you know what tests he or she is planning to set so you can plan your own timetable accordingly and test the effectiveness of your revision.

You should make sure that your timetable includes at least eighteen hours' personal revision a week. You can then get an overall view of your workload during the weeks leading up to the exam. Figure 1 gives an example of a revision timetable. You can see that this particular student doesn't mind working all week but likes Saturday and Sunday completely free. You may prefer to schedule your time differently.

Next construct a second revision table along the lines of Fig. 2 for each of the topics you intend to revise and the days on which you will try and cover them. You can simply tick them off as you complete the revision. This student who is studying statistics has for one reason or another chosen to leave out certain parts of the syllabus. Perhaps the student does not feel that he or she can allow sufficient time for effective revision of every topic.

3. General tips. As you put your revision plan into operation the following tips will be useful.

(*a*) If you fall behind on your schedule catch up on it by the end of the week even if it requires additional work.

(*b*) Set yourself an objective for each session or, if you are taking internal examinations, ask the tutor to set you an objective for your intended revision plan for that week or day, e.g. to understand a particular topic, cover a certain amount of work or take a test.

(*c*) As soon as you settle down start work. Getting started is always the most difficult part.

(*d*) Rest for a few minutes approximately every twenty minutes and simply think about what you have just read. Break for twenty minutes approximately every $1\frac{1}{2}$ hours. At this point you might find it relaxing to take some refreshment or chat to someone about something else or do something completely different like listen to a record.

(*e*) Whenever possible do not study late at night. Keeping regular sleeping hours and being ready for a full day's work the next day is important, so stop at least one hour before your usual bedtime and do something you enjoy.

III PLANNING FOR REVISION

Subject: Statistics

Week one	
Monday	No revision
Tuesday	Collecting data and analysis
Wednesday	Presentation of statistical information
Thursday	Regression and moving averages.
Friday	No revision
Saturday	No revision
Sunday	No revision
Week two	
Monday	No revision
Tuesday	Correlation
Wednesday	Averages.
Thursday	Probability
Friday	No revision
Saturday	No revision
Sunday	No revision
Week three	
Monday	No revision
Tuesday	Probability (continued)
Wednesday	Sampling Theory
Thursday	Significance tests.
Friday	No revision
Saturday	No revision
Sunday	No revision
Week four	
Monday	No revision
Tuesday	Indices
Wednesday	Dispersion
Thursday	Standard deviation
Friday	No revision
Saturday	No revision
Sunday	No revision
Week five	
Monday	
Tuesday	
Wednesday	
Thursday	
Friday	
Saturday	
Sunday	

FIG. 2. *A subject revision table.*

(*f*) If your revision is all reading rather than writing you will find it helpful to sit where you are most comfortable—even if this is in an armchair with your feet up—though many people find it easier to concentrate at a desk or table. Remember you will need good lighting from behind.

(*g*) Above all, develop the right attitude towards the revision that you are going to do. Think that you have only got so many weeks to revise and in this time you are positively going to enjoy coming to terms with the subject for what may be the final time.

If you think about it, most of these tips will apply whether you are revising for a written exam or practising a piece for an exam in dance or music.

WHERE TO REVISE

4. Revision at college. Some revision such as laboratory work is obviously better undertaken at college but the following tips show how the principles of college-based revision can be useful for other work as well.

(*a*) Sitting next to a student who is very good in a particular subject is useful. You can often improve your own performance and also that of your fellow student who may gain further insight into the subject as he tries to explain it to you.

Remember, though, that your task is to pass the exam, not compete with the other students in your class, so don't waste time trying to outdo others; work *with* them instead.

(*b*) With this last comment in mind you can form brain-storming groups at college to tackle certain tasks (*see* V, **3**). For instance, a few students could look at a question together and within a given time—say ten minutes—outline from their discussion the way they think the question should have been answered and why. Later, in the revision class, they can check with their tutor to see whether their conclusions were correct.

(*c*) If possible sit close to the front of the class where you have a greater opportunity to hear and see as well as ask questions.

(*d*) Most tutors are prepared to help students who try hard. You may find it useful, therefore, to ask your tutor if he or she will mark any work you complete on your own outside class and go over with you the reasons for the marks awarded.

5. Using libraries. You should make use of your college or local library throughout your course as it is an ideal place to carry out research, extended reading, tracking down references, etc. It is worth knowing how to get the most out of your library—the information available, the type of indexing systems used and how to operate microfiche machines etc. The library assistant will be only too glad to help you.

Libraries are also useful during revision time for certain aspects of your work.

"Are you quite sure you don't want the library to provide cushions?"

(*a*) Quick reference is possible where a part of the subject has slipped your memory.

(*b*) Where the exam takes the form of an assessment of a thesis or the composition of a dissertation or report, a library containing original works is of paramount importance.

(*c*) Where you are taking the final exams of a professional body, for example, which requires you to be conversant with the latest developments in the field, reference to a selection of specialist books and periodicals is essential.

(*d*) A library is often the only place where many students can find a quiet and warm place to study.

OTHER ASPECTS

6. Handwriting. If necessary throughout the revision period try to improve your handwriting until it is completely legible. You may well lose marks if the examiner has difficulty reading your handwriting.

7. Revision equipment. Unless it is a practical exam there are very few items that you will need for revision, but you should have:

(*a*) at least three coloured pens;
(*b*) two pencils and a rubber;
(*c*) a ruler;
(*d*) an A4 ring binder and writing pad with punched holes;
(*e*) if allowed in the exam room a calculator, log book or slide rule (if you are entered for a numerical subject).

All your notes should eventually be filed in the ring binder, but take only the writing pad when you travel to your place of revision as the loss of the ring binder would mean the loss of your complete set of notes.

CHECKLIST

1. Draw up a weekly timetable for all subjects to be revised.
2. Draw up a complete revision timetable for each subject.
3. Plan your revision to coincide with the lectures and/or revision at your college.
4. Start improving your handwriting if necessary.

CHAPTER IV

Actual Revision

"Thinking means connecting things, and stops if they cannot be connected."

G. K. Chesterton

INTRODUCTION

1. General. If you have worked hard until this point you may only have spent a couple of days to make sure that you have all the basic facts and equipment that you need to get down to revision.

If your revision time is limited select for revision only those topics in which you do not excel and that occur regularly in the examination. If you have sufficient time to revise the whole syllabus, then again, start with the topics which you find the most difficult, thus allowing enough time to make sure that you completely understand them.

2. How long to revise. If you have been really sensible you will have allowed approximately six to eight weeks for revision. Starting sooner may mean that the tutor has not yet completed the syllabus and you will become bored by the continual effort of revision over a lengthy period. If you have allowed less than six weeks you are cutting it fine unless you have taken very good notes throughout your course (*see* **5–6** below) and obtained above average coursework results.

TESTING YOURSELF

3. Examination tests. It is critical that you set yourself a test (mock examination) each week that relates to the requirements of the examination. This applies whether it is a written, numerical, oral or practical examination.

To structure one of these tests is simple and in IX you will be given advice on how to be successful in a test or examination, so read this before setting yourself such a test.

Try to set yourself the test on the day that you are not revising, possibly Saturday or Sunday daytime.

To set yourself the test you should first work out the following facts.

"I told him he was trying a three-hour test too early in his revision programme."

(a) Determine how many topics you think you have learnt well during the previous week.

(b) Check how long you would be allowed in the actual examination. For instance, it may be that the actual examination allows you 3 hours to answer 5 questions, so by dividing 3 hours by 5 you will find out the time required for completing each essay.

Given this information, if you are going to attempt in your test three questions, the time that you should allow to complete the test is (3 hours ÷ 5) × 3 = 1.8 hours, or 1 hour 48 minutes.

(*c*) Obtain some examination type questions that relate to the topics from any or all of the following sources:

(*i*)   past papers,

(*ii*) text books, or

(*iii*) tutor.

(*d*) Begin testing yourself.

Train yourself for the examination, just like an athlete for a race. Start, for example, by doing a test the first week for two hours, and work up each week until you can complete the test in the time allowed in the actual exam approximately one week before the exam is due to take place.

4. Analysis of test performance. After you have finished your mock exams or any tests you have set yourself ask yourself the questions given in Fig. 3. Complete the scale by putting a ring around the appropriate number that you feel reflects the way you performed, then join up the points you have ringed. Read all the questions before you attempt to answer.

If your scale shows a profile tending to the right-hand side like that given in Fig. 3 then you are on the right lines but have little cause for complacency. Where the points do not fall on the right-hand side work on correcting that element immediately, but remember that the importance of each element listed increases as the exams approach.

Scales of this type indicate where you are going wrong, and once you have done this exercise a couple of times you will find yourself doing it in your head after each test or exam and before the next. If you are taking a series of final examinations it is a good idea to construct a graph for each exam.

TAKING NOTES

When you are revising is not the time for lengthy note taking or copious copying. At this stage you should make only brief essential notes so that any spare time may be used for thinking about the topic. However, before making any fresh notes check what you wrote down during your course to see if the information is complete. The following paragraphs give advice on effective

IV ACTUAL REVISION

EXAM SUBJECT: *Sociology*.

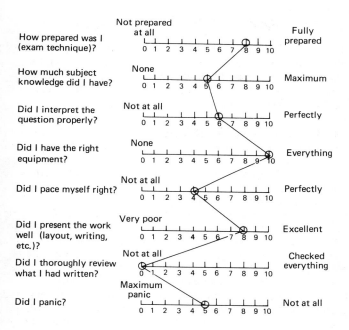

How prepared was I (exam technique)? — Not prepared at all 0 1 2 3 4 5 6 7 8 9 10 Fully prepared

How much subject knowledge did I have? — None 0 1 2 3 4 5 6 7 8 9 10 Maximum

Did I interpret the question properly? — Not at all 0 1 2 3 4 5 6 7 8 9 10 Perfectly

Did I have the right equipment? — None 0 1 2 3 4 5 6 7 8 9 10 Everything

Did I pace myself right? — Not at all 0 1 2 3 4 5 6 7 8 9 10 Perfectly

Did I present the work well (layout, writing, etc.)? — Very poor 0 1 2 3 4 5 6 7 8 9 10 Excellent

Did I thoroughly review what I had written? — Not at all 0 1 2 3 4 5 6 7 8 9 10 Checked everything

Did I panic? — Maximum panic 0 1 2 3 4 5 6 7 8 9 10 Not at all

Additional comments/observations:

Spent too long on first question. Had to race through rest and therefore didn't have time to read work done. This caused some panic.

From textbook question 4 was interpreted wrongly.

FIG. 3. *A scale showing performance in a test (refer to* **4** *on p. 20).*

methods of taking notes. (Further advice may be found in *Use Your Head*, T. Buzan, BBC Publications.)

5. How to take notes. Effective note taking is related to the way you personally see things and generally speaking each student's notes are only completely logical and understandable to that particular student. When you reread your notes they should remind you of the main topics and provide the trigger for further thought on the subject.

Some rules for good note taking are given below and illustrated in Fig. 4.

(*a*) Write down only the key points or phrases that the tutor or book covers. Don't get bogged down by small detail. Your thoughts should be concentrated on formulating argument and opinion backed up by facts relating to the most important aspects of the subject. If the small detail is frustrating, don't waste too much time trying to understand the point. Ask your tutor later to explain it to you.

(*b*) Space your notes out so that you can easily find a particular topic on a page or add more information at a later stage.

(*c*) Carry a small notebook with you to jot down any points that may suddenly occur to you.

(*d*) Use diagrams and illustrations wherever possible (*see also* **6** below).

(*e*) Make sure you make complete references to chapters in books and articles that you have read in case you need to refer back to them later.

(*f*) Making notes should *follow* your reading. Do not make notes whilst you are reading, but read small but complete sections at a time instead.

Figure 4 gives an example of notes taken for an economics topic which has four key factors. The student has made use of both (*a*) written and (*b*) diagrammatic forms which should preferably be on separate A4 sheets of paper. The written notes may include specific information such as dates, quotes, examples, definitions, etc. These notes are obviously incomplete suggesting that there was insufficient time to cover the entire topic in the class period, but notice that in the written notes in particular plenty of space has been left to add further information at a later stage.

FACTORS OF PRODUCTION - lecture 1.

Ref: TEXTBOOK OF ECONOMICS - J. HANSON
     Pub: Macdonald and Evans   (chap. 3).

GEN INTRO:
Collective description of individual elements that
contribute to production of goods or services.

AIM:
Greatest output from input of f. of P.

Contrast profit aims with social aims.
F of P = Land, Labour, Capital + Entrepreneurs.

LAND:
Def: Resources made available by nature
inc: land (above and below) sea and air.

SUPPLY can fluctuate re: underground water found
irrigation.

LAW OF DIMINISHING RETURNS OPERATES (gen)
optimum production per unit of resource then
decline. Req and of other factor (s).

RENT

FIG. 4(a).   *Notes made in written form.*

6. Diagrammatic notes. Students do not often make use of
diagrams when taking notes, but they can be a very effective
method for a number of reasons.

(a) Our brains like to see things in shapes or patterns and we

23

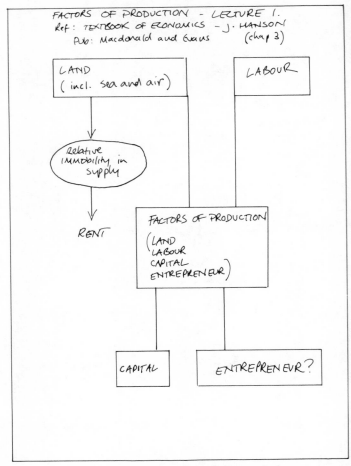

FIG. 4(b). *Notes made in diagrammatic form.*

can remember patterns more readily than abstract entries or designs.

(*b*) By using diagrams the importance of individual notes can be put in perspective.

(c) Diagrams allow plenty of space for additions at any point.

(d) You can see immediately an overall picture of the topic under consideration.

(e) Diagrams help visual recall of a topic at revision time.

When presenting notes in this way start by placing the main theme of the topic at the centre of the page so that you can then move in any direction (*see* Fig. 4(b)). It is also an advantage to use colours when taking notes in diagrammatic form.

CHECKLIST

1. Set yourself a test each week.
2. Check your performance in your tests each week and work to improve your weak areas.
3. Ensure that your note taking is efficient, economic and effective.

CHAPTER V

Studying in Groups

"Education must have an end in view, for it is not an end in itself." Sybil Marshall (from *An Experiment in Education*)

1. Introduction. Studying in groups is generally encouraged in courses of higher education but there are benefits to working in groups at all levels.

The purpose of working in a group is to develop a wider and deeper understanding of a topic through the pooling and questioning of ideas. Studying in a group also helps to improve your ability to answer examination questions precisely as you are continually being required to justify your position on a topic to other members of the group.

Study groups usually come under five main headings, although for revision purposes the first three (**2–4** below) are probably the most useful. The value of group studies cannot be emphasised enough in developing a student's knowledge of a subject and his or her ability to analyse a subject and work with others.

2. Discussion groups. These may be formal or informal.

(*a*) *Formal* discussion groups usually require the election of a chairman and speakers for and against the motion.

(*b*) *Informal* discussion groups, however, are more useful for revision purposes as they may take place at any time and in any place. All that is required is a few fellow students who are prepared to hold a constructive and free ranging discussion—not argument—on a specific topic or question. Members of the group must realise that the point is to approach a problem on various levels and from different points of view, not to win an argument.

3. Brainstorming sessions. Brainstorming groups are a little like an enforced discussion. As time may be short during the revision period it may not be possible to hold a free ranging discussion, so each member of the group is expected to contribute in the following stages of the session.

(*a*) First present as many facts and ideas on a topic or question as can be thought of within a given amount of time.

(*b*) Again within a specified amount of time, extract the major points relating to the topic or question from the pool of ideas amassed at stage (*a*).

(*c*) Finally, discuss, select and agree on—even by a vote—which way the problem or question should have been resolved or answered.

4. Study groups. Study groups are more useful in project or case study work where a group is formed to examine a case, complete a project or resolve a problem, e.g. on urban development, international relations or how to launch a new product.

Quite often it is possible for a class to have several separate groups working on exactly the same problem and then each group presents its conclusions to a panel of experts who determine how each group has performed.

Study groups are invaluable for students who have to take mini-case or case study examinations.

5. Role playing. In role playing situations a group of students work towards the solution of a problem by each playing a role so that the procedure simulates a possible real-life situation.

This can be a very exciting method of learning subject matter as well as learning how to handle awkward situations. However, due to their complexity such sessions are used more extensively during the course rather than during the limited time available for the revision period.

6. Seminars. These are very useful in developing students' ability to analyse, but like role playing they are normally established and conducted by the tutor within the confines of the classroom.

Seminars are basically discussion groups whose purpose and

momentum are controlled by the tutor. It is usual for the lecturer to seat the students in a half-moon arrangement with the tutor seated in the centre at a point visible to all.

CHECKLIST

1. Study in groups whenever possible.
2. If your tutor is willing arrange role playing sessions and seminars to develop your abilities to handle awkward situations and analyse problems.

CHAPTER VI

How to Remember Information

"Everything should be made as simple as possible
—but not simpler."

Albert Einstein

INTRODUCTION

1. Remembering. The things we remember with ease are those
we come across time and time again—our face in the mirror, our
telephone number, our home address. This simple fact of
familiarity is central to the learning process—to learn we must
remember and to remember we must make ourselves familiar
with the subject in question.

This is the aim of your work throughout your course, and the
aim of your revision should be to consolidate your knowledge.
However, one problem most of us find is remembering information relating to a topic we have only been able to study for a short
time and are not thoroughly familiar with. Ways in which we can
help ourselves to achieve that familiarity, then, form the basis of
this chapter.

2. Methods of remembering—mnemonics. There are a large
number of methods around for helping us to remember and any
device to aid the memory is known as a *mnemonic*. The most
effective are:

(a) good note taking (*see* IV, **5–6**);
(b) objective tests;
(c) picture association;
(d) word association.

The latter two methods have the advantage that they can be practised and repeated anywhere, even while travelling.

OBJECTIVE TESTS

3. Objective tests. These are a part of many exams so it is vital that students should understand what they involve. Essentially, an objective test consists of questions that the examiners believe can have only one answer.

NOTE Objective tests are further covered in VII.

EXAMPLE

Tick the appropriate answer

1. Tripoli is the capital of:
   - Luxembourg
   - Austria
   - Libya
   - Iraq

2. New York is the most highly populated city in the world: Yes_____No_____

3. The height of the Eiffel Tower to the nearest metre is: _____metres

4. $5 \times \frac{3}{7} + 7 =$ _____

You will see from this example that objective test questions may be set in a number of different ways of which those above are only a few. Others require the student to answer questions against a written passage which must be quickly read and memorised and is taken away before the student starts answering the questions set against the passage. Another type of objective test question presents a selection of diagrams or words and the student has to select the diagram(s) or word(s) that are similar or next in the sequence. (This type of question is often used in IQ (Intelligence Quotient) tests.)

Any or all of these types of objective test questions may be used to help you remember the subject you are revising.

4. Setting your own objective tests for revision. Once you have your notes write a set of objective test questions down the left-hand side of a piece of paper. Leaving plenty of space write in your answers on the right. (Do all this in neat handwriting as you may find it more convenient to ask someone else to read the questions to you.) In this way you can cover the answers with a blank sheet of paper and expose the relevant answer once you have tried the question.

Before you actually compile your questions quickly reread your notes to remind yourself of the whole subject so that you can put your questions in the right order. Don't dwell on this exercise—it should only take you a few moments to think of the layout for each question.

Once you have compiled your set of questions test yourself—or have someone else test you—at every available opportunity.

NOTE It is not always necessary to construct your own objective tests. For many subjects books of such tests are available from good educational bookshops.

PICTURE ASSOCIATION

5. Picture association. This method is becoming increasingly popular but is mainly of use for remembering one or two words at a time.

Think of an object you are bound to or probably will see every day such as a particular shop or a bus or type of car and link the word you wish to remember with that object. It doesn't matter how stupid, absurd or simple the link, but it does help if it is amusing. From then on every time you see that object you will recall your phrase or saying linking the object to the word you are trying to remember, though it may be wise not to say anything out loud or you may get some peculiar looks from other people! If you wish you can also link the object and word to the subject to which it relates.

EXAMPLE
Suppose you are studying economics and need to remember the terms *supply* and *stock*. Following the method outlined above you might make up the following:

On seeing an optician's shop	— *Supply* my eye it's *economic*
On seeing a lingerie shop	— I wonder if they *stock* stockings

You do not always have to see the object in order to be reminded of the word you are trying to remember. For instance, in the above example you do not necessarily have to see an optician's shop to bring the word *supply* to mind. You could simply imagine yourself in front of an optician commanding him to "*Supply* my eyes". Alternatively you might imagine a short, heavily bespectacled optician reaching up to place an enormous pair of glasses on your head. This would obviously appeal if you were tall and didn't wear glasses!

A similar technique may be used to remember a *list* of words.

EXAMPLE

Suppose you are a medical student and need to remember the following list:

1. Sun and Vitamin D
2. Arm
3. Antibiotic and penicillin
4. Dilation
5. Cranium

These may be linked by picture association together with a few words to visualise the situation as follows.

"*One Vitamin D* comes to you from the *sun*." As the body generates Vitamin D in sunlight, imagine someone lying in the sun with the letter D continuously rising from his or her body.

"*Three anti-biotics* and sister *peni-cillin*." Imagine introducing someone to your three grotesque Aunty Biotics and your sister Penny Ceiling. If the words are slightly different it doesn't matter as long as they are sufficiently similar to bring to mind the actual words.

After memorising a list in this way ask a friend to test you by giving you a number in the list to which you have to give the answer. You'll be surprised by the number of items you can remember.

6. Diagrammatic notes. We have already covered notes in diagrammatic form in IV, **6**. However, once you have completely revised a subject it helps to make another diagram putting the name of the subject at the centre and arranging the main topics and sub-topics around it on branches. This provides an excellent last minute reference before the examinations and will also help you to memorise the whole subject.

EXAMPLE
Figure 5 illustrates the use of this technique. In the diagram the ovals represent the main topics and from them branch lines indicate sub-topics and other related factors. This has been completed for the main topic Factors of Production. Note how

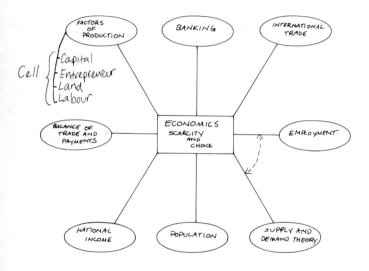

FIG. 5. *Diagrammatic notes as an aid to revision.*

the sub-topics have been listed in such a way as to make a *mnemonic* CELL (*see also* **10** below).

Where topics may be interrelated dotted lines can be used to indicate the relationship, as shown between Employment and Supply and Demand in Fig. 5.

If you are studying economics you might like to try completing the diagram. Of course, the same approach can be used for any subject. A last minute look at your diagram before you leave for the examination is a speedy way to refresh your memory.

WORD ASSOCIATION

7. Rhymes. During the course of our education we have all made use of rhymes to help us remember facts and figures, for example:

"I before E except after C"

"Thirty days hath September, April, June and November etc."

Welding students could find the following rhyme useful for remembering the words in italics:

Acetylene is a *gas*
That has a little *smell*;
With *oxygen* and a *torch*
You'll *blow* yourself to hell.

A similar method can be used for remembering formulae. Consider the following formula used in statistics for determining two unknowns:

$$\Sigma y = an + b\Sigma x$$
$$\Sigma xy = a\Sigma x + b\Sigma x^2$$

These may be remembered by the following rhyme:

Why a bax and not
a bx²?

This should prompt you to recall from your actual studies the positions of these letters in the equation and where the additional terms (the Σ (sum of), the extra x and the n) should be placed.

8. Stories. Making up a story can often help you to remember lists of facts and figures.

EXAMPLE

You have to memorise the following countries and their capitals:

France	Paris
Austria	Vienna
Norway	Oslo
England	London

The following story may help:

"I went to *Paris* for *French* champagne and *Vienna* to ski in the *Austrian* Alps, but then I just had to go to *Oslo* to swim in the *Norwegian* fiords. Eventually I missed *London* and had to return to my home in *England*."

9. Sequences. These are a familiar method of helping to memorise information. Obvious examples of a sequence are the multiplication tables we used to learn at school:

Once two is two
Two twos are four
Three twos are six, etc.

This principle can also be applied to words we need to remember in a sequence. If we create a sentence from words which begin with the same letters as the words we are trying to remember we can also remember the sequence they should be in. (The method can also be used for any list of words which do not need to be in sequence.)

EXAMPLE
You have to learn a list of place names in the order in which they are distant from London. The top line below makes a sentence with the first letter of each word matching the town it stands for:

Could	Better	Machines	Last	Eternally
Coventry	Birmingham	Manchester	Liverpool	Edinburgh

A similar method of substitution may be used to help remember and distinguish between words. For example, to remember the distinction between "stationary", i.e. not moving, and "stationery", i.e. paper, pens, etc., think of the saying "Envelopes are stationery". Envelopes are indeed stationery and the "e" the word commences with will remind you that the word "stationery" is also spelt with an "e".

10. Making up words. One of the easiest ways of all to remember lists of facts is simply to take the first letter of each of the words you have to remember and make them into another word.

EXAMPLE
Suppose you have to remember the four types of questions that may be used in questionnaires as listed below. We can arrange them as shown so that the first letter of each spells the word MODS. When we recall the mnemonic MODS we are then reminded of the words we have to remember.

*M*ulti-choice questions
*O*pen ended questions

Dichotomous questions
Semantic differential scales

This technique can often be used in many situations and in conjunction with other techniques, as we have seen in **6** above on diagrammatic notes.

"Business Buses Break Bus Stops . . ." *"Eh?"*

11. Remembering languages. When you have to learn a European language such as French or Spanish it often helps if you can refer back to any Latin you learned at school. Alternatively, you can relate the foreign word you are trying to remember to an English word or situation or write a sentence in English incorporating the word to help you remember it.

12. Swot cards. These are pocket-sized cards carrying the most important information on a subject or topic, usually in note form. Because of their size and durability you can carry them with you all the time so that you can revise virtually anywhere.

VI HOW TO REMEMBER INFORMATION

Most subjects are covered by one publisher or another, but any educational bookshop will be able to tell you if they are available for your subject. Students often compile their own—good revision in itself!—and frequently amend them. In this way over a period of time they become an excellent revision pack to carry with you.

REMEMBERING SHAPES

13. Pictures, photographs and maps. To remember items that are simply a shape, e.g. a photograph showing the layout of internal human organs, it will help if you try to make it form a pattern. You will find this easier if you work from a major point in the map or photograph.

EXAMPLE
Suppose you have to remember a map. The overall shape may be that of a light bulb, so you might say to yourself:
"That map lights up my life . . ."
The main point on the map may be a bridge that crosses a river, and both the bridge and the river are to be found a quarter of the way up from the bottom of the map. You might then say to yourself:
"That map lights up my life . . .
. . . but it only goes a quarter of the way to bridging my thirst."
Now, we have used the words "lights, quarter, bridging and thirst" to help us remember the shape of the map and its major points, the position of the bridge and the river.

14. Filling spaces. Objects can also be easily remembered by mentally placing them in some orderly fashion such as arranged in an imaginary empty room or around a hall or field. Then, when you are in the examination, recalling the room or field will bring the objects to mind.

CONCLUSION

15. Summary. By now you will have seen that most things can be remembered using one or a combination of the techniques we have just outlined. If you can, make your main method of recall one which your friends or relatives can help you with. People who care about your success will always help you to save a lot of time by, for example, reading to you your objective test questions or making up rhymes and sentences for words you have given to them. In fact, you may find that they become so interested that they start asking what the words mean, and having to explain them to someone helps you to understand your subject even more!

If you find suddenly during the examination that there is something that you cannot remember it is best not to let your mind just go blank as some people suggest. After all, it may not come to you at all, and meanwhile time is passing. Instead, try going back to first principles at the heart of the subject and work back to the point you wish to figure out or remember.

Remember, most of these methods of committing information and facts to memory can be done outside the actual revision time you have allocated for learning and taking notes. Use these techniques to make your revision periods an enjoyable way of life and not a chore.

CHECKLIST

1. Set yourself a series of objective tests as revision practice.
2. Use the methods outlined in this chapter for memorising your study material:
   - picture association
   - diagrams
   - rhymes
   - stories
   - sequences
   - making up words
   - swot cards
   - image patterns
   - filling spaces

CHAPTER VII

Objective Tests Revised

"Human history becomes more and more a race
between education and catastrophe."

H.G. Wells

INTRODUCTION

1. General. Students who are about to sit an "objective test" as part or the whole of an examination will by now appreciate the types of questions which may be included in the exam (*see* VI, **3-4**). It is beyond the scope of this book to discuss the validity of such tests as assessments of the ability of the examinees concerned, but the tests do exist and they are, in certain cases, extremely useful. In view of their popularity, therefore, we will consider them further in this chapter.

The test may fall into any or all of the categories outlined in **2-6** below.

CATEGORIES OF OBJECTIVE TESTS

2. Recall/comprehension. This usually involves reading a passage or article on a particular subject and then answering a selection of questions on the content of the passage without being able to refer back to it.

3. Numerical ability. Although such tests come under the heading of mathematics few require detailed workings, and indeed little space or time is allowed for working the answer out in "longhand". The questions may cover arithmetic, geometry, algebra, statistics, etc.

Normally the answer can be worked out in the head as the examiner is really testing the speed with which the examinee can interpret the relationship between figures and manipulate them without putting pen to paper.

4. Data evaluation. This involves either reading a passage containing a lot of statistics or other information or studying tables, charts or graphs and then answering problems which require some sort of evaluation of the data studied. Alternatively you may be required to apply the data to a given situation to achieve a certain goal. You may or may not be allowed to refer back to the data when answering the questions.

5. Grammar and its usage. As this implies such questions directly test the examinee's knowledge of grammar and its usage.

6. IQ tests. IQ (Intelligence Quotient) tests may consist of questions from all the categories outlined above plus others designed to test the examinee's ability to interpret a variety of relationships, sequential and non-sequential, between a number of items such as pictures, diagrams, numbers, letters or words.

PRACTICE AND REVISION

7. Practice and revision. The best way of revising objective tests is to practise them as often as possible. Past papers and books of objective tests are easily obtainable, and most reputable educational bookshops will stock the more popular IQ tests.

Objective tests generally assume you have the knowledge already and they are really testing the speed with which you can apply it. Other types of test assume no previous knowledge but assess your level of intelligence from the number of questions you have been able to answer in the time allowed. In this type of test with a given level of intelligence you should be able to answer all the questions.

Obviously, for most tests, a good command of the language in which the test is set is critical for success. However, the checklist given below may give you a few tips to help you with your revision practice.

CHECKLIST

1. Make sure you fully understand the overall format of the test, how it is given and how long each section ought to take.

2. Read the directions on the test paper very thoroughly as you will probably not have time to make changes. Objective tests usually stick rigidly to times for individual sections, unlike essay type exams where you can catch up later if you took too long over one of the essays.

3. Always put yourself under strict test times when revising as you are trying not only to improve your comprehension but also the speed with which you comprehend.

4. If you feel certain about an answer don't ponder on it. Accept that you have got it right and move on to the next. This is particularly important where the answer is achieved by pure deduction, as in mathematical questions where only *one* answer can be correct.

5. If necessary take an educated guess. However, before you do this, bear in mind what marks may be deducted if you are wrong. For example, if it is 4 marks for a correct answer and 1 mark for the rest take an educated guess, especially if you are certain that two of the answers are incorrect.

6. Leave difficult questions that are holding you up until you reach the end of the section, particularly if they carry the same marks as other questions. Remember the question may only be difficult for you. In this way you will be gaining marks for the majority of questions which you have been able to answer correctly before returning to the few you found difficult.

7. If you avoid a question make sure that subsequent answers are given to the correct question number. Do not put the answer to Question 5 against Question 4 because you have left Question 4 out.

8. Above all, keep the three Ps in mind—
   PRACTISE
   Don't PANIC
   PACE yourself well

CHAPTER VIII

Word Power

IMPROVING YOUR READING SKILLS

1. Fast reading. It is essential to realise from the beginning that fast reading is not necessarily *effective* reading. Judges, for example, are among the slowest readers among the professions both in their work and personal lives. What is more important than sheer speed is that you understand, absorb and remember what you are reading.

2. How to improve your reading. Few people read *efficiently*, gaining the maximum benefit from the time they spend engaged in reading. Attention to the points listed below will help you improve your reading skills considerably.

(*a*) *Develop the right mental attitude.* Before you read something, e.g. a chapter in a textbook, take the attitude that you are going to enjoy what you are about to read and find it interesting. If you look on your reading as a chore that is exactly what it will become.

(*b*) *Read in blocks.* Don't read as if you were looking at each word individually. Try to take in the meaning of a sentence or paragraph as you read so that you read the chapter as interrelated sections each making a specific point. Practice at increasing your span of comprehension will also increase the speed at which you read.

(*c*) *Read it twice.* Read each chapter at your usual reading pace then stop for a while and read it again more slowly, concentrating on the points that you didn't quite understand during your first reading. If after three attempts you still cannot understand something leave it until you have an opportunity to discuss it with your tutor and move on to something else so that you do not become discouraged.

(d) *Read before the lecture.* Whenever possible read about the topic *before* the lecture so that you can follow it more easily and discuss any problems with your tutor. If you do your reading *after* the lecture you may come across things you don't understand and not have the chance to sort them out with your tutor.

(e) *Make notes.* After the second reading make notes summarising the main points and listing the questions you wish to ask your tutor. It also helps if you underline what you consider to be key aspects of a chapter in relation to the examinations.

(f) *Don't read for too long.* About twenty to thirty minutes of concentrated reading is enough at one time. Have a rest for a few minutes before you return to the text. Always stop before you become tired.

(g) *Reading position.* Whenever possible read in natural light but make sure that the light is coming from behind you so that it does not shine in your eyes and give you eye strain.

(h) *Don't pre-judge.* Approach your reading with an open mind. A set opinion about the topic before you begin reading will prevent you from appreciating the points made by the author. Try to read other authors on the same topic to give yourself a variety of viewpoints from which you can judge the subject.

(i) *Read more.* The more you read the more your reading skills will improve. Try to get into the "habit" of reading—this will be very useful throughout your life!

(j) *Improve your vocabulary.* It cannot be stressed enough how important a good vocabulary is, not only for more effective and enjoyable reading but also for interpreting examination questions correctly. The following sections deal with this important aspect and give some advice on how to increase your word power.

IMPROVING YOUR VOCABULARY

3. Word power. It cannot be emphasised enough how important it is to be able to understand exactly what the words used in setting exam questions actually mean. A wider vocabulary will also be extremely useful for presenting your answers to particular types of topic or argument.

Unless you are perfectly clear what particular words used in exam questions mean you may find yourself during an exam thinking that you cannot answer all of the questions you are asked. This of course means you are losing marks unnecessarily simply because you are unsure about what is required in the answer. These following paragraphs are designed to help you increase your vocabulary and so avoid such a situation.

4. Increasing your vocabulary. One way to increase your vocabulary is to ask your tutor to give your class ten words each week throughout the year which are related to the subject being taught. The following week one of you should explain to the rest of the class what one of the words means, another of you should then explain one of the other words and so on. About eight weeks before the exam it is a good idea to start including particular words that have actually appeared in previous examination papers.

The following list gives some examples of the type of words you should be looking out for and what you should be understanding by them.

Example	*Understanding*
Abstract	Summary; divorced from reality.
Allude	To refer to indirectly.
Anarchy	Absence of government.
Chronicle	Record of events.
Collusion	Secret agreement between persons usually with the intent of doing wrong.
Evaluate	To determine the value, worthiness of the item, action or proposition.
Generic	Something pertaining to a class or group.
Intransigent	Refusing to compromise.

You can also compile your own list, but as there may not be much time before your exams a small selection is given below for you to study and commit to memory. It is a good idea to carry a small pocket dictionary with you so that you can not only analyse this list but also any word that you come across that you don't understand. In particular you should look out for words that relate to your subject. Don't be surprised if you find that your initial understanding of the word doesn't agree with that of the

44

dictionary, but once you fully understand what each of the words means place them in a sentence to practise your understanding.

aggregate	criticise	finite
antithesis	describe	function
atrophy	differentiate	gambit
carnivorous	discuss	incumbent
comment	dissect	infinite
compare	disseminate	integrate
concave	dissertation	portfolio
concur	dissipate	potential
confer	distribute	receptive
consequence	diverse	regressive
consider	elicit	reiterate
context	entreat	retrospective
contra	evoke	rural
contrast	exponential	significance
convex	extrapolate	thesis
correlate	factor	

5. Using your vocabulary. Although you should be trying to increase your vocabulary and your understanding of words it is always sensible *not* to use long words in an effort to impress where short simple words will explain what you mean just as well. Long words generally have several interpretations and their continuous use tends to break the natural flow of your essay. This can make it difficult for the examiner to read and creates a bad impression.

Long words should only be used where there is no suitable alternative. If used sparingly they will add to the essay rather than confuse your meaning.

CHECKLIST

1. Improve your reading skills so that you read efficiently with the minimum wastage of effort and time.
2. Improve your vocabulary and understanding of words that frequently appear on examination papers.

Students' Queries:
Revision Time

Q: As a married person with children I can't get enough time to revise due to my responsibilities within the family. What can you suggest?

A: It's difficult for married people to find sufficient time to study, but many do accomplish it and find the rewards at the end make it all worthwhile.

At the commencement of the revision period discuss the work effort required with your partner and ask if he or she could take more of the domestic work-load during the revision period. It may, for instance, be a good idea to go directly to a library from college and work until it closes and then go home and relax or do something else for the rest of the evening.

If you do encounter resistance try inviting some friends around from your course who are worried about the pending examinations. They, without being asked, may convince your partner about the amount of work needed. If all else fails remember that you should take the decision as to a course of action in the light of how beneficial exam success will be to the family unit.

Don't forget at the end of your examinations how hard it has been for your partner to tolerate you during your study periods.

Q: What should I do if I find at the commencement of the revision period that the tutor has not fully covered the syllabus?

A: If the examination has been set by the tutor then there isn't too much to worry about.

If, however, the examination is externally set there are four courses of action possible.

(i) Discuss it with the rest of the class and then discuss it with your tutor as a group. He may have just overlooked that particular part of the syllabus because he is new to teaching that particular course.

(ii) If (i) is not successful discreetly bring it to the attention of the Course Tutor.

(iii) If (i) and (ii) are not successful and you are still worried you may be able to arrange for personal tuition on the topic.

(iv) Failing the above courses of action study the topic independently and then discuss it with fellow students to ensure that you understood the reading material.

You will usually find that courses (iii) and (iv) are rarely necessary.

Q: Can you suggest places to study?

A: Almost anywhere is suitable for studying depending on what you are studying. Simple memorising for instance can be done whilst travelling, in a hotel foyer or waiting room.

Studying that requires deep and lengthy periods of concentration should, however, be done where quiet can be guaranteed for some time and where it is warm but well ventilated.

CHAPTER IX

The Examination—Presenting Your Work

"I think—therefore I am."
Descartes

TYPES OF QUESTIONS

1. Introduction. When writing an essay it is important to understand exactly what the examiner requires you to do. A well designed question paper will indicate through the words used in the questions what sort of answer the examiner is seeking.

Most question papers and even individual questions fall into one of two very general categories:

(a) *Descriptive*; or
(b) *Analytical*.

2. Questions descriptive in nature. This type of question may commence in the following ways:

1. Describe . . . .
2. Define . . . .
3. Outline . . . .
4. State . . . .
5. What do you understand by . . . .
6. How would you . . . .
7. Show how . . . .
8. Explain . . . .
9. Distinguish between . . . .

When questions beginning in this way do not ask you to do anything further it is expected that the answer will provide a full account of the subject matter in essay form but not an analysis. This may possibly include some or all of the following aspects:

(a) a definition of the topic;

(b) a description of the relevant points that relate to the topic;

(c) the importance of the points mentioned which may include their application with regard to the item in question;

(d) where possible, support the points mentioned with your own "made up" but correct examples or "actual examples". This may include diagrams, illustrations or graphs;

(e) if necessary show how the item being written about differs (can be distinguished) from other items that are very similar.

EXAMPLES

Q.1 Define mammals and describe how they feed their young. Use illustrations in support of your explanation.

Q.2 Outline the major training aspects to consider when designing a training programme.

Q.3 (a) Outline the elements of a binding contract.

(b) Mr Smith purchased a car from a Mr Brown who, in passing, informed Mr Smith that he was a trader. Mr Brown claimed that there was "nothing at all wrong with the car". Mr Smith purchased the car and shortly afterwards found that the brakes were in a dangerous condition. Advise Mr Smith as to his legal position.

Q.4 (a) Define inflation.

(b) Discuss the economic consequences of inflation in a mixed economy.

You will notice that the second part of Questions 3 and 4 are analytical (see 3 below) in nature and require students to use more than their memory or simple deduction. The parts containing the words "outline" and "define", being mainly descriptive, would receive less marks from the examiners, perhaps just 25 to 40 per cent of the total marks awarded for the question. (Some examining bodies help by indicating the marks to be awarded to each part.) The student should, therefore, allocate his or her time accordingly when answering such questions and restrict the answers to the descriptive parts to one or two paragraphs.

3. Questions analytical in nature. These questions may commence in the following ways:

1. Discuss . . . .
2. Analyse . . . .
3. Evaluate . . . .
4. Comment on . . . .
5. Contrast . . . .
6. Criticise . . . .
7. Compare . . . .
8. Assess . . . .
9. Consider . . . .
10. Argue the case for/against . . . .

These types of questions generally require the student to:

(a) show within the first paragraph that he or she clearly understands the whole question and set up the framework the student is going to adopt for the rest of the essay;

(b) provide the arguments for and against or state the advantages and disadvantages unless specifically asked to adopt a point of view for or against a proposition;

(c) handle the major elements of the topic as early as possible in the essay;

(d) provide, where possible, supporting facts, cases or examples;

(e) arrive at a considered opinion in favour of or against the proposition under discussion or conclude (if justified) that insufficient evidence is available to arrive at a firm opinion/conclusion, unless, as in (b) above, specifically asked to adopt a point of view.

EXAMPLES

Q.1 It has been argued that violence in society increases with increasing unemployment. How far do you support this contention?

Q.2 War is the inevitable outcome of failed politics. Discuss.

Q.3 Assess the validity of the claim that permissiveness in society erodes moral values.

Q.4 Argue the case for the existence of God.

4. Combined questions. Sometimes questions involve both aspects, descriptive and analytical or applied, without being in separate parts.

EXAMPLES

Q.1 Describe and analyse the methods used by governments in controlling the freedom of the media.

Q.2 Define social mobility. How may a knowledge of social mobility help in re-housing people?

5. In-between questions.

1. List . . . .
2. Briefly explain . . . .
3. Note the . . . .

Questions that commence in this way are usually a part of a larger question. Such an introduction indicates that considerable lengthy explanations are not necessary. In the case of "briefly explain", for instance, a paragraph would probably be all that is necessary.

EXAMPLE

Q.1 (a) Outline Rank and Pearson Product–Moment methods of correlation.

(b) The following tables detail the exam results in percentages of students studying two subjects. What is the correlation between their results in the classes?

Maths class (24 students*)			*Physics class* (24 students*)		
%	%	%	%	%	%
A 39	J 49	S 67	A 33	J 55	S 70
B 41	K 52	T 68	B 50	K 55	T 77
C 44	L 53	U 69	C 50	L 47	U 80
D 44	M 53	V 70	D 41	M 70	V 61
E 45	N 56	W 78	E 43	N 66	W 69
F 46	O 58	X 80	F 46	O 68	X 76
G 46	P 59		G 60	P 64	
H 46	Q 65		H 40	Q 65	
I 47	R 65		I 48	R 72	

*Each student is indicated by a letter of the alphabet.

METHODS OF MARKING

6. Playing the examiner. Examiners *are* human and try to mark as fairly as possible in difficult circumstances (*see* also XIII). To help you appreciate the examiner's problem put yourself in his position. Read the question below and then the ways in which six certificate level advertising and marketing students have started to answer it in the twelve minutes that they were allowed for writing their introduction. At the end of each one, award a mark out of 10 based on your feelings concerning the attempt. Don't worry about passing or failing each student, just give a mark which you honestly feel correct. You don't have to know the subject.

"Half the money spent on advertising is wasted." Discuss.

Student No. 1

Advertising is often used synonymously. Advertising includes all activities which attempt to inform the public about the firm. This also includes public relations.

The role played by advertising in the marketing activities of a firm varies greatly. Advertising can be direct or indirect. The object of most advertising is to present information about a product.

I think in a large organisation the management spends money on advertising to promote the business. If an organisation spent half the money on advertising it is not a benefit for the firm, because the organisation cannot stand firmly in the market.

Award a mark out of 10 here _____

Student No. 2

If the originator of this statement had used the word "some" instead of "half" and defined the use of the word "wasted" then he or she may have had some justification in forwarding such a sweeping and yet absolute statement. But this is not the case and therefore it must be rejected.

To determine, if indeed, any wastage occurred it would first be necessary to determine all the original objectives of advertising and consider how effectively these have been achieved. The businessman may consider that no wastage has occurred if there is a profit obtained from the advertising investment. On the other

52

hand the accountant may see the matter in strictly cost terms whilst the corporate planner would evaluate the indirect long-term benefits.

Award a mark out of 10 here _____

Student No. 3

If half the money spent on advertising is wasted depends on the product which the factory or company wants to sell.

In the world there are many products and different companies. If the advertising is completed and the company has success I think the money isn't wasted and each product has its life duration, and each country has its . . .

Award a mark out of 10 here _____

Student No. 4

The money which is wasted in advertising is because of the persons who deal with the advertisements in the advertising department did not think carefully how to protect their customers buy putting advertisement.

By placing an advertisement its very important for new goods, especially because by advertising the public would know. But if there was no advertisements how comes the public know about it.

Award a mark out of 10 here _____

Student No. 5

It is doubtful if the person who made this statement could find any research to support the idea that exactly half the money spent on advertising is wasted. In any field of social science it is rare to find such absolute claims.

Such a statement is analogous to statements like, "Half the people in the world are stupid." How can it be exactly one half and by what criteria is "stupid" determined? A closer analysis of the objectives of advertising and its direct and indirect returns will illustrate that such a statement may be accepted or rejected depending on the view of the advertiser and the goals he wishes to achieve.

Award a mark out of 10 here _____

Student No. 6
To get a new product off the ground, to have a sizeable share in the market for indentical goods, some form of advertising is absolutely essential. Any costs incurred in such advertising is usually planned with time and space.

In the age of telecommunications e.g radio, telephone, T.V, etc a lot of people can be made aware at the same time without having to deal with them individually. It all depends on the advertiser to condense all available information necessary to influence the huge audience bearing in mind the absolute utility and its advantages over identical but alternative goods. Money spent on advertising. . . .

Award a mark out of 10 here _____

7. Analysing your reactions. You will probably have considered the efforts of Student No. 2 and Student No. 5 to be the best. If you have not, then let some of your friends try and you will probably find a pattern of marking that supports these findings.

If we analyse why 2 and 5 were considered better than the others we may discover what mistakes were made by the others and help ourselves avoid similar mistakes in our own work.

These would probably be the general findings of discussions regarding the introductions presented by Students 1, 3, 4 and 6.

(*a*) *Several did not appear to know how to start.* They seemed to be fumbling around writing what they knew about the topic ignoring the key points of the question.

(*b*) Having started, several appeared to be *illogical* in their presentation.

(*c*) A couple, such as Student 1, wrote in the first person, i.e. "I think . . .", instead of remaining *objective* in approach, i.e. "It would appear . . .".

(*d*) Several did not appear to have thought out what they were going to say. They probably did not prepare an *essay plan*.

8. Why were 2 and 5 successful? The result of discussions on the success of 2 and 5 could probably be summarised as follows:

(*a*) They approached the first paragraph from a global point of view showing that they understood the question before going into detailed reasoning.

(*b*) They set up the framework by which they would answer the question indicating that they were not unduly influenced by the statement as presented by the question.

(*c*) They immediately attempted to answer the *key points* in the question.

9. Presentation. You may have been able to tell that these introductions were written by overseas students, hence the problems that some had with spelling and grammar. Examiners will often be understanding of the difficulties encountered by such students whose first language may not be English, but not if the essay is illogical in its presentation or lacks clarity. In this respect the introductions of Students Nos. 3 and 4 would probably not pass any examination above a very basic certificate level.

How to construct an essay and the various approaches which may be used to achieve this are outlined in **10–14** below.

WRITING AN ESSAY

This brings us to the next aspect in writing essays. How to actually write an essay and the various approaches that may be adopted.

10. Components of an essay. Usually, good essays have:

(*a*) an interesting beginning;
(*b*) persuasive content; and
(*c*) a conclusion.

"Usually", because good essays may take many forms. Nevertheless, here we are attempting to formulate a style that will help ensure a pass so we will concentrate on the most popular approaches.

11. Interesting beginning. As pointed out before (*see* **8** above) introductions should:

(*a*) go to the heart of answering the question;
(*b*) indicate the examinee's overall attitude to the question asked;
(*c*) approach the answer to the question in a general global way.

To illustrate this aspect of the essay look back to the introduction of Student No. 5. He has clearly shown that he has analysed the "key" words in the statement (namely, "half the money") and may not agree with the originator of the statement.

In the second sentence he explains his reasoning for the contention he forwarded in the first sentence. He continues this justification at the beginning of the second paragraph.

In the latter half of the second paragraph he then indicates that more facts and reasoning are required. These he is going to produce in the rest of his essay to support this view.

12. Persuasive content. A persuasive content depends on the amount of facts the student produces to support his comments and, in particular, the amount of reasoning he provides. This does not mean that the essay should contain every fact that the student can remember. It is more essential to select three to five major facts in relation to the question asked. The facts should also support your reasoning, not the other way round.

13. A conclusion. Normally, the final paragraph is reserved for concluding the essay. This does not necessarily mean that you have to agree or disagree with any proposal that may be suggested by the question. There may be as yet insufficient facts to justify either agreement or disagreement.

Although the final paragraph is really rounding off the essay, you would be well advised not to start your final paragraph with the words "In conclusion . . ." or "Finally . . ." as this rigid approach does not find favour with most examiners.

14. Example of a good essay. The following essay illustrates the approach outlined above and was written by a student taking a coursework test. He achieved nearly 90 per cent for this essay; the 10 per cent was lost because he did not include in his essay all the information that the examiner was seeking at that particular level of work.

Example of an
applied analytical type question

QUESTION
A small company employing forty people produces a product for industrial users and another for the general public. Discuss the ways by which you may advertise these products.

ANSWER

A company which employs only forty people will have certain
limitations in so far as its ability of production is concerned and
also in how much money it has available to use on advertising.
This means that the company cannot afford to launch a
massive advertising campaign all over the country and possibly
abroad and even if it did manage it somehow it would not have
the facilities to cope with the large increase required in output.

The product the company is manufacturing for industrial
use would need to use specific media in order to achieve
optimum results and these media could be discovered by
market research. However, market research can prove to be
very expensive and when weighed up with the amount of
money available for advertising may not prove to be a practical
step to take. The company would therefore use the more
obvious media such as trade journals, direct mail, trade shows
and exhibitions and perhaps the business sections in national
newspapers. Trade journals would probably be used as these
will reach the specific market that the manufacturer wants to
reach. The advert must show that the product the firm is
making can help other industries in making a profit, either by
saving time, making something more efficient or whatever the
benefit is. A trade fair or exhibition is also an ideal means to
both advertise his product and also to sell it. The advertising
part comes from his very presence at an exhibition as well as
editorial write ups and possibly an advert in the exhibition
catalogue.

With a small firm of around forty people it is probable that
there will be a good after sales service due to the company
being of a personal nature resulting from its size. This could be
included in any advertising.

A product for sale to the general public, from the same firm
would need a completely different set of media, although
again, the luxury of market research would be too costly. Here
the company must decide on the best media for advertising its
product. If it is sold in shops, in the high street say, he can
advertise it at point of sale effectively by getting show cards
printed or display stands made. If it is decided that television
advertising is out, and it probably will be, then there is the
small ads in the national press. The company must determine
to what type of person it is selling its product in order to know

what is the best newspaper to place ads in. For instance, the popular newspapers appeal to lower economic classes than do the quality newspapers. If its market is more localised, as it quite likely is with a small firm then its best medium will be local newspapers which have the best circulation of any local media, or posters on local billboards or possibly even advertising on local cinemas. Another possibility is to post leaflets through letter boxes in the immediate area of the business, if that is where the company thinks its market lies (e.g. a printers or bakers).

With advertisements to the general public the copy should contain less technical jargon and should only point out the main benefits to the consumer.

Advertisements for the product to industry can show more technical information as this is what the prospective buyer understands and wants to assess.

The main consideration with advertising both products to both the markets is one of what the company can afford in relation to what it considers the most effective promotional mix and if they can they produce enough to cater for increased orders.

ESSAY STYLES

15. General. It is worth noting that a good style will produce an essay that is logical in content and structure which will be easily understood by those who read it. There are many essay styles but the most popular are outlined in **16–19** below.

16. Style 1. In this style there is a recognisable pattern: introduction, content and conclusion. Usually in using this style the student argues points for and against throughout the whole essay.

For example, in paragraph two of the suggested answer given in **14** above the student contended that market research would be advantageous and then went on to limit this statement by suggesting that the company may be too small to afford market research.

The *advantages* of this style are:

(a) such essays are usually interesting and stimulating to read;

(*b*) if the student does not have time to finish the essay the examiner can see that he was capable of analysing the subject.

The *disadvantages* of this style are:

(*a*) such essays are more difficult to write and are more appropriate for analytical rather than descriptive types of questions;

(*b*) they place more responsibility on the examination marker who has to assess the relative importance of the key points that the student has raised in his answer.

17. Style 2. Here the student uses approximately half the essay to present his discussion from one point of view and then the rest of the essay for presenting the opposing points.

As an example consider the following question:

"Discuss the advantages and disadvantages of a public school education."

Using this style the student would spend half the essay presenting the advantages and then the rest of the essay presenting the disadvantages.

The *advantages* of this approach are:

(*a*) it is easy to present;

(*b*) the examiner can clearly recognise the points raised in the essay.

The *disadvantages* of this approach are:

(a) it is rigid in style;

(*b*) it is not so interesting for the examiner to read as Style 1.

EXAMPLE

What are the advantages and disadvantages of women going out to work?

SUGGESTED ANSWER

The advantages and disadvantages of women going out to work vary greatly depending on the circumstances of the individual. Indeed, even societies and groups within societies differ in their opinion depending on their social and cultural background. This lack of resolute opinions on the subject is partly due to the subjective judgments that are involved. Nevertheless, if a survey of opinions were undertaken the following would probably be found to be considered the major advantages.

When women go out to work more money is received in the household. This affords a higher standard of living for all concerned which in turn may improve standards of hygiene and education.

If a country is not fully utilising its natural resources then the employment of more women may help ensure that the wealth in such resources is released for the benefit of the whole society. Also, there are talents of women that are not being used because insufficient women go out to work.

For women a major social benefit must be the added freedom of action and independence that they may enjoy from having an income of their own.

A major benefit to society as a whole is the increase in the disappearance of sex discrimination which frustrates and annoys many women as well as causing an unjustified elitist attitude in men, an attitude that can cause destructive social friction at all levels.

It may also be argued with justification that as women more fully understand the needs of women in our society they should be in the corridors of power where they can represent such interests in order to work towards a more equitable society.

Advantages, however, also imply disadvantages which often balance up the argument.

One disadvantage which applies to women with families is that most persuasive and yet contentious argument that the quality of family life must suffer when married women go out to work. Children are deprived of full mother care and guidance that helps form an emotionally stable and balanced adult. It is argued that this cannot be effectively substituted by others caring for the children while mothers are away at work.

Where a country does not have enough work for everyone it would be more sensible for women to remain at home thus ensuring the security of jobs for men whilst fulfilling an equally if not more important role within the household. This balancing of supply and demand for labour would also assist in maintaining high wages instead of the frequent exploitation of people at work.

As women often only spend part of their adult life at work

they deprive many men of an education or training that they would use on a continual basis rather than stopping, sometimes for years, to bring up children.

Increased income for the household can sometimes give way to materialism and people may substitute material possessions for personal relationships and communication which are so valuable in developing a humane society.

You may have noted in the above example how the student changed the direction of the essay by the "link sentence" that constituted paragraph seven. He was then able to introduce the disadvantages that were requested by the question. There could also have been a conclusion but as an opinion was *not* requested the student is justified in answering solely what was asked.

Having read this controversial essay you are probably straining to voice your disagreement with some of the points mentioned. It is worthwhile mentioning, therefore, that it is the *force* of your argument that examiners are generally marking, *not* whether you agree or disagree with their personal judgment on the subject. The student who answered the question in the example above would not necessarily have lost marks for the comments in the second half of the essay even if it had been marked by an ardent feminist! Exam markers always attempt to remain objective and without bias when marking.

In the descriptive type of questions, however, often it *is* possible to have a definitive answer which the examiner is expecting as this type of question basically tests the knowledge that a student has about a topic rather than his judgment.

18. Style 3. In this method the student highlights the major points that he is considering throughout the essay as in the following example in which the paragraphs have been indicated with a letter of the alphabet. The advantages and disadvantages of this approach are as in **17** above and both approaches tend to be adopted more by students who are at a certificate level in their education.

EXAMPLE
(*Descriptive type question*)
What do you understand by a take-over bid?
List the circumstances which give rise to the making of a take-over bid.

SUGGESTED ANSWER

A "take-over" bid is the name given to the technique whereby a company or financial group makes a general offer to the shareholders of another company to purchase either the whole of their shares or enough to give control of the company in question. In some cases bidders will negotiate with the directors of the company they seek to take over and induce them to recommend the acceptance of the offer to the shareholders. If the support of the directors cannot be obtained, the bidder may approach the shareholders directly.

The circumstances which give rise to the making of a take-over bid include the following:

(a) Where the bidder is of the opinion that the management of the company is not sufficiently vigorous, and the bidder believes that he can achieve a larger return from the assets involved than is the case at present.

(b) Where the directors have pursued an unduly conservative dividend policy resulting in an artificially low price for the shares.

(c) Where the business will benefit from inclusion in a larger group of companies by means of the economies of scale, etc.

(d) If the business owns property, the bidder may intend to increase the return from the property by putting it to an alternative use.

(e) The company may have cash reserves which the bidder wishes to control in return for shares or stock in the merged company.

19. Style 4. A further style is to present the less important points first and then build up to the major points.

The *advantage* of this approach is that it is interesting to read. On the other hand, the *disadvantage* is that if time runs out the student may not get the chance to present the most important aspects of the essay.

In the following example the student brings out what he considers to be the major points in the final two paragraphs.

EXAMPLE

Argue the case for the abolition of television.

SUGGESTED ANSWER

There are two main objections to television. The first is an objection to the presence of television itself within the home because many people are prone to compulsive viewing. Secondly there are those who object to the use to which such a persuasive and influential medium is put. With these points in mind it is appropriate to question the material that we are given for viewing albeit by a state-controlled or commercial channel.

It would probably be fair to claim that ninety per cent of the programmes are concerned with entertaining. Even current affairs and news programmes are more concerned with the size of the audience they attract rather than the unbiased presentation of information that would develop the audience's awareness of all aspects of life.

The rest of the programmes that fall within this area of viewing are mainly concerned with titillating the curious, escapist or materialistic side of people's natures with the likes of soap opera series, adventure films or contests in which there is a financial reward.

Even in countries where the state is in total control of the television media the viewer is subjected to numerous boring one-sided documentaries designed to influence society towards one opinion or another and encourage it to support the current body of bureaucrats in the office of government.

The organisers' traditional and commercial view of what people want to watch causes them to present programmes that play down to that element in us that guarantees audience figures thus preventing the development of competent acting and original works.

Where advertising is involved the viewer is subjected to an advertising language full of clichés and is encouraged to buy goods and services which may not be needed. It is often the case also that advertisers can dictate which programmes will be shown and the moral tone of the programme, particularly in America.

In addition advertisers seek to influence children without the presence of their parents in the hope that they will request their parents to buy the particular item being advertised.

Many of the products advertised are also dangerous for the health of the populace such as cigars, alcoholic drink and what is termed "junk foods" and yet strong controls over advertising them are rarely introduced.

But if there was one element of television that would justify its abolition on its own merit it would be the intrusion television makes into the fabric of family life. Television involves more of our senses than radio or newspapers and thus we become less able to undertake other activities. Family games and interests that were enjoyed together are replaced by blank stares by all concerned towards one corner of the room or derisive arguments arise about what programmes should be watched. This destroys the kind of communication within families that develops togetherness and helps prevent them from following pursuits that involve and develop them personally rather than the personalities on television.

It is easy to claim that we have choice but when we are subjected to this inane treatment from childhood it becomes difficult to make sensible choices later in life, even the collective, and sensible choice to abolish television.

You may feel that the student who wrote this essay has been unfair and one-sided but remember that he was asked to argue the case for abolition, not to make comments that may be construed as presenting the opposing argument.

20. Other essay styles. The essay styles in **16–19** illustrate the main ones used in examinations requiring analytical or factual answers, but there are others. Even those shown may be mixed when answering certain questions, particularly where the question is in two or more parts with each part requiring a different approach. Likewise, Style 1 in **16** could have been used in answering the question regarding the advantages and disadvantages of women working posed in **17**.

There are also other types of question that specifically ask for your opinion, such as:

"What in your opinion is the most important issue of our time?"

In this case you are justified in writing in the first person at some point in the essay. Usually at the beginning, end or both.

Other types of questions may require little or no facts or analysis. The examiners are more concerned with assessing the examinee's literary flair and imagination.

EXAMPLES
Write an essay on either:

The strangest event that may happen to a person.
or
An unexpected meeting.

Obviously, the answers will probably be completely fictitious. No example is given for these types of questions so that the reader is not tempted merely to copy rather than exercise his or her own imagination.

21. Summary. In general, the question will suggest the style to adopt for your answer. If, however, your examinations are internally set and marked you would be well advised to ask the views of your tutor (*see* **26** below). On the other hand, if you are sitting external examinations the examining body may supply specimen answers or Examiners' Reports indicating their preference.

Bear in mind that the further you progress in your academic studies the more you will be expected to avoid a rigid approach when writing essays.

ESSAY PLANS

22. The reason for an essay plan. Essays that do not appear to have any sensible direction or form are usually the result of unplanned writing. Before you begin writing think about the question for a few minutes and make some notes. This advice cannot be stressed enough.

In most exam papers you will also find that the instructions anticipate that you will be preparing these notes and advise you to put a cross through them and start your question on a fresh page. Many students, despite having read these instructions, completely ignore them and start each answer directly after the previous one. Many marks could be lost through poor presentation creating an adverse image of the work in the mind of the person marking the scripts.

23. What is an essay plan? An essay plan consists of the brief notes made on one complete page of the examination paper which reflect the major points and approach you are going to use in the essay. You should, therefore, write it down during the five minutes you allow yourself before each essay to consider what the question is asking and how it should be answered.

Before commencing the essay, plan what you are going to write as follows.

(*a*) Read all of the question paper very carefully!

(*b*) Give a star rating in order of importance to the questions that you believe you can answer.

(*c*) Number the essays in the order that you intend to answer them.

(*d*) Commence with the essay for which you believe you could gain considerable marks because you know the subject well.

In the example of an examination paper given in Fig. 6 the student has indicated with a star his question preference and the order in which he intends to answer them, namely 7,6,3,5,1. By doing this the student knows that his weakest work will come last, which is important in case he does not finish the whole examination paper. If there had been a compulsory question on the paper he would, of course, have started with that one.

Illustrated in Fig. 7 is an essay plan for the complete essay given in **14** above. As you study this plan see how it relates to the actual written essay. A considerable space has been left between the notes made relating to each paragraph so that additional points may be added if you decide that they are necessary as you write the essay.

24. How an essay plan helps. An essay plan will help you in the following ways.

(*a*) You will be able to see the scope of the question at a glance. Once you have constructed the essay plan, look back over it and ask yourself if the answer you intend appears balanced. If not, make adjustments and additions until you are satisfied.

(*b*) The essay plan will help you to keep to the point by forcing you to consider the key points of the question as you make notes for each intended paragraph.

Look at the example examination paper in Fig. 6 and you will see that once the student had decided the questions to answer he underlined the key parts of the question so that he could refer to them throughout as he writes his essay plan.

(*c*) An essay plan will improve the speed at which you write the

INSTRUCTIONS TO CANDIDATES

SUBJECT: Business Administration

TIME ALLOWED: Three hours

Answer FIVE questions only.
ALL questions carry equal marks.

5 ✗   1.   <u>Why</u> should a company <u>formulate objectives</u>? Give <u>examples</u> of the <u>objectives</u> a company may have and <u>discuss</u> the <u>relevance</u> of those you have chosen.

✗   2.   What are the functions of management? Discuss the elements and the relevance of these management functions to a company.

3✗✗   3.   What <u>factors</u> in the <u>environment</u> have an <u>impact</u> on the <u>company</u>? <u>Describe</u> how these factors <u>influence</u> the <u>company</u>.

✗   4.   "Marketing is a key function in the organisation." Discuss this and state how it is related to other functions.

4✗✗   5.   What are the <u>functions</u> of the <u>financial department</u> in a company? Discuss the <u>nature</u> and <u>place</u> of <u>cash flow statements</u> in the company <u>operations</u>.

2✗✗✗   6.   "<u>Production management</u> is concerned with <u>planning and control</u> of <u>production.</u>" Discuss.

1✗✗✗   7.   "<u>Personnel management</u> is a <u>functional</u> area of <u>management</u> as well as the <u>responsibility</u> of every <u>line manager.</u>" Discuss.

✗   8.   "Research and Development should be given terms of reference." Discuss.

FIG. 6.   *An examination paper marked up for preferences by the student.*

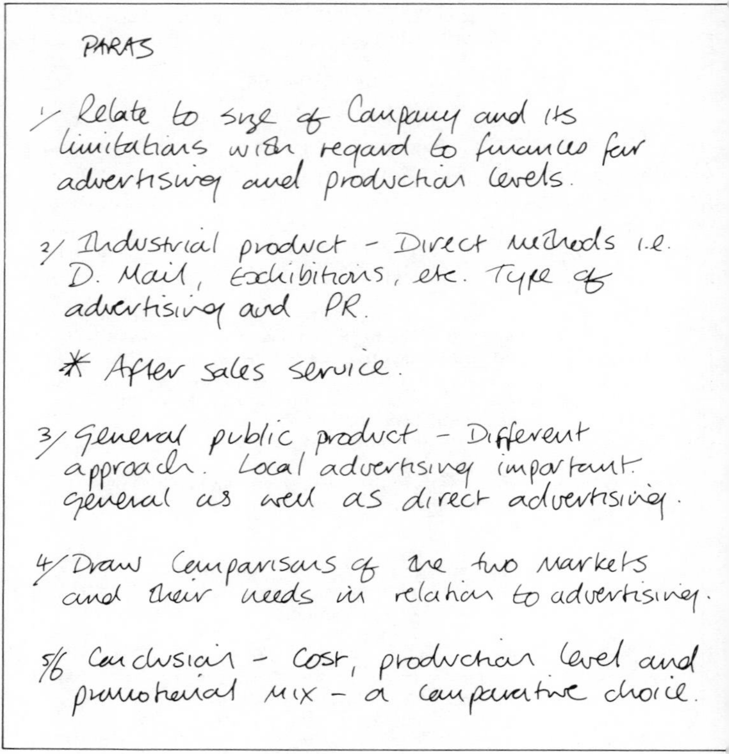

PARAS

1/ Relate to size of Company and its limitations with regard to finances for advertising and production levels.

2/ Industrial product — Direct methods i.e. D. Mail, Exhibitions, etc. Type of advertising and PR.

* After sales service.

3/ General public product — Different approach. Local advertising important. General as well as direct advertising.

4/ Draw Comparisons of the two markets and their needs in relation to advertising.

5/6 Conclusion — Cost, production level and promotional mix — a comparative choice.

FIG. 7.   *The essay plan for the essay given in* **14**.

essay because you know precisely what you are going to write, thus saving you time in contemplating each paragraph.

(*d*) If you do not finish your final essay the examiner can see from your notes what you were going to write. He would take note of your rough work at his discretion, but at least it would be there should he choose to be lenient in the event of your overall marks being border-line.

However, if you are definitely going to run out of time, it will be easy for you to take the points from your essay plan and neatly write them in note form so that the examiner can see how you intended to complete your essay.

Do not forget, however, to cross through all your rough work and start the essay itself at the top of a separate page.

CONCLUSION

25. Pacing yourself. Many students, because they have been praised for outstanding essays in one or two topics during their coursework, mistakenly believe that they will easily pass the whole examination. However, it is better to obtain average marks across all the topics in a subject than to be outstanding in only a few.

As an example look at the marks awarded to two students who had taken a final examination. Student A did not have time to complete the final essay as he had spent so much time on the first two. The marks are for the five essays that each attempted.

		Student A	*Student B*
Essay	1	16	$10\frac{1}{2}$
	2	14	11
	3	$8\frac{1}{2}$	$9\frac{1}{2}$
	4	6	10
	5	4	11
	Fail	$48\frac{1}{2}\%$	*Pass* 52%

These students' marks also illustrate the following points.

(*a*) You should try to pace yourself in the examination so that you spend an equal amount of time on each essay. This can be best achieved by practice.

(*b*) You can acquire this practice by taking any *mock* exams that your tutor is willing to set during your revision.

26. Personal preferences of tutors. Should you use the essay style most favoured by a particular tutor in an examination, even if a different style comes more easily to you, especially if it is an internal exam and that particular tutor will be marking the essay?

This is a common dilemma faced by students. Unfortunately in the circumstances the safest course of action is to adapt your essay style to the preferences expressed by the tutor if you are to increase your chances of success, though of course any style of writing as implied by the question itself should bring success if it contains good reasoning and is supported by appropriate and convincing facts.

If, however, the exam is set externally then you should always aim to answer the question in the style implied by the wording. (*see* p. 48). Nevertheless, examiners will always make allowances for unusual essay styles provided they are effective, well reasoned and fully supported by appropriate facts.

CHECKLIST

1. Practise writing essays.*
2. Present your tutor with each essay that you write and ask for his or her opinion.
3. To develop flexibility try writing in each of the styles illustrated in this chapter.
4. In the exam make relevant markings on the question paper so that you know which questions you are going to answer, which order you will answer them in and what the key words are in each.
5. Always make an essay plan before you begin to write.

*If you can, study *Effective Teaching* by Elizabeth Perrott (Longman's). Although mainly a book for tutors it gives excellent coverage of the various types of exam questions. There are, however, no specimen answers.

CHAPTER X

Numerical Work and Illustrations

"The aim of education is the knowledge, not of facts but of values."

W.R. Inge, Dean of St Paul's

1. Numerical questions. Many students lose all their confidence when confronted by questions which involve the manipulation of numbers. Such anxiety is really unnecessary as this type of exam is in a sense easier to pass than an essay type of exam as the questions usually have only *one* correct answer. This means that the examiner has to mark your answers much more objectively since to arrive at the correct answer you must follow a particular series of predetermined steps. In addition, the fairness of the marking can easily be checked after the exam, particularly if it is an externally set exam and the examining body publishes model answers.

2. Rough workings. As with essays you must show any rough work you carry out, and it is important that you keep this rough work quite separate from your actual answer to avoid confusion. If the examiner marks your rough work by mistake instead of the full answer you will lose many vital marks!

When you are setting out your answer it is also advisable to provide an explanation of what you are doing at every stage. By doing this you will be showing the examiner that you know what you are doing and why you are using a particular formula. In this way, even if you arrive at the wrong answer, at least you have shown that you knew how to approach the question and will pick up some marks for that knowledge.

3. Presentation. It is important to bear in mind that neat handwriting and the effective use of language are also important in numerical exams, particularly if the exam has a written element. In fact, neatness of layout and presentation are vital if you are to convince the examiner that you know what you are doing and convey the correct answer.

This approach also applies to any diagrams or graphs which may be included in your answer. If they are neat and tidy you will be able to include all the necessary information in a clear and unambiguous manner.

4. Illustrations. Diagrams and graphs should only be included when they are asked for in the question or when you are sure that they will help to explain the subject matter more clearly. If in doubt it is best to leave them out. It is worth remembering that although you will pick up marks for a good illustration, you could also lose marks if the diagram is inappropriate, gives the wrong information or is untidy.

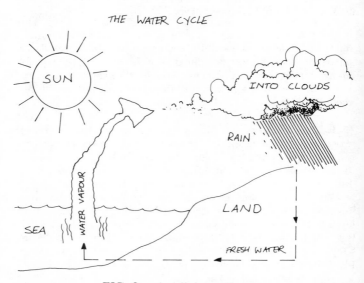

FIG. 8. *A well drawn diagram.*

When drawing your illustration make sure it is large enough so that you can explain on it what each element shown represents. Many students make the mistake of drawing the diagram so small that there is no room to provide an effective description. Plenty of paper is available in an exam so use it if you need to. In general it is best to allow a third to a half of a page for each diagram to give yourself enough space. Figure 8 demonstrates these points for an illustration drawn in answer to a question on the water cycle for a biology exam.

Similar advice applies to graphs if you are supplied with separate sheets of graph paper (*see* the graph included in the model answer given in Fig. 9).

If you are likely to have to draw illustrations in your exam make sure you take with you a ruler and a compass (a coin is also often useful) so that you can draw your diagrams neatly and effectively.

5. Example. Figure 9 gives a student's answer to the question posed below and illustrates all the points covered in this chapter on neatness of presentation and the size and purpose of diagrams.

QUESTION

Graph the figures given below for Company **X** Ltd and determine using first linear regression the sales they may reasonably expect from an advertising expenditure of £8,000.

Previous advertising expenditure (£000s)	Resulting sales (£000s)
8.7	89
6.9	74
7.1	71
9.4	97
9.7	95
8.5	87

6. Conclusion. It is always worth remembering that you don't have to get everything right to obtain marks. If the answer to the question given in **8** above was being marked out of 100 and the student had got a column wrong in the table then he would probably have only lost a maximum of 5 marks.

TABLE TO DETERMINE SUM TOTALS FOR THE EQUATIONS

Previous ADV. EXP. £000's x	Sales Resulting £000's y	x^2	xy
8.7	89	75.69	774.3
6.9	74	47.61	510.6
7.1	71	50.41	504.1
9.4	97	88.36	911.8
9.7	95	94.09	921.5
8.5	87	72.25	739.5
50.3	513	428.41	4361.8
Σx	Σy	Σx^2	Σxy

Y will be found when $x=7$ and $x=9.5$ for determining the 1st linear line on the graph. 'a' and 'b', the unknowns, will be determined by using the simultaneous equation :-

$\frac{1}{2}$ $\Sigma y = na + b\Sigma x$
$\frac{2}{2}$ $\Sigma xy = a\Sigma x + b\Sigma x^2$

Therefore, substituting the totals into this equation, we have :-

$\frac{1}{2}$ $513 = 6a + b \, 50.3$ (x eq 1 by 8.383 to clear 'a')
$\frac{2}{2}$ $4361.8 = 50.3a + b \, 428.41$

8383 was obtained from dividing Eq. 2 'a's by Eq. 1's a's. Taking Eq 2 from Eq 1 to clear 'a's we have :

$\frac{1}{2}$ Now equals $4298.94 = 50.3a + b \, 421.51$
$\qquad \qquad \qquad 4361.80 = 50.3a + b \, 428.41$
$\qquad \qquad - \; 62.86 = \qquad \quad b - 6.9$

$\therefore \; b = -\dfrac{62.86}{-6.9} = 9.11$

Returning b (9.11) to the formula (1) to find 'a' =

$\therefore \quad 513 = 6a + 9.11 \times 50.3$
$\qquad \quad 513 = 6a + 458.23$
$\qquad \quad 513 - 458.23 = 6a$
$\qquad \quad \dfrac{513 - 458.23}{6} = a = 9.13$

Using the formula $Y = a + bx$
For entering on the graph to determine trend
let $x = 7$ and 9.5 s.t. formula

$$\therefore Y = 9.13 + 9.11 \times 7$$
$$Y = 9.13 + 63.77$$
$$Y = 72.9$$

$$\therefore Y = 9.13 + 9.11 \times 9.5$$
$$Y = 9.13 + 86.55$$
$$Y = 95.68$$

DETERMINING EXPECTED SALES FOR COMPANY X FOR ADVERTISING EXP.
OF £8000.

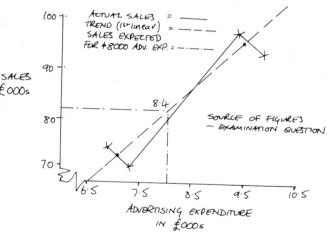

ACTUAL SALES = _____
TREND (1st linear) = - - - - -
SALES EXPECTED
FOR £8000 ADV. EXP. = -·-·-·-

SOURCE OF FIGURES
– EXAMINATION QUESTION

SALES
£000s

ADVERTISING EXPENDITURE
IN £000s

Reading from the graph, expected sales may
be approximately <u>£84,000</u>

FIG. 9.   *A student's model answer.*

CHECKLIST

1. Explain any workings in your answer.
2. Only use diagrams and illustrations if they help explain the subject under discussion.
3. Allow one third to half a page for each diagram or a page of graph paper when drawing graphs.
4. Make sure you enter all the information required on your diagram.
5. Neatness of presentation is of vital importance.

CHAPTER XI

Case Studies, Mini-cases and Reports

"All education is, in a sense, vocational—vocation
for living."

Sir John Newsom

1. Introduction. Gaining in popularity with examining boards
are questions set against an imaginary situation (case). The
student must read, analyse and answer questions based on the
information given in the case. Mini-case histories tend to cover
one or two pages whereas a full case study may be anything from
ten to thirty pages.

A full case study cannot be reproduced here but by analysing
the requirements of mini-cases we will understand what will
probably be expected in a case study examination.

MINI-CASES

2. Types of mini-case. There are generally two types of
mini-case. One sets questions about a situation based on a specific
topic that the student is studying. The other gives a general
situation and the questions could be on any topic within the
subject area.

In mini-cases on general topics the examiners are wanting to
discover how well the student can integrate his knowledge on
several subjects to resolve a problem. Many examiners consider
that this is a better test of a student's ability because it forces the
student into the position of a person actually responsible for a
decision and calls on *all* his knowledge to provide a reasoned
answer.

The following example illustrates both approaches. In a

general type of mini-case the study could have been on almost any aspect of life.

MINI-CASE

Wheelers Cars Ltd

Wheelers, a well established car distributor, had a total of five large showrooms located on prime sites in major cities throughout the UK. They were, in fact, main agents in the five cities for an up-market German car.

When the economy was buoyant sales went well but with the onset of a recession the company is faced with major problems. In general, sales of the German cars are falling, consequently the amount of service and maintenance work that is done by the garages attached to the showrooms is also falling.

George Carter, previously a sales manager of a larger car distributor group, has just taken over as Managing Director, Mr T Race the previous Managing Director having just retired. Having had an opportunity to examine the various aspects of the company he has called a directors' meeting to discuss the current position of the company and prepare a plan of action to rectify matters.

Mr Carter first explained the general condition of the company and then dealt with the question of the Birmingham showroom.

"It would appear that the company has only £100,000 cash on deposit of which £20,000 is already accounted for if current debts were to be paid. Debts to the company are virtually non-existent as either the customer or HP company settles the cost of the car at the time of purchase.

"The company has approximately sixty cars paid for in stock. The reason that they are paid for is because with sales so slow the cars have had to be paid for before they were sold. The value of these cars if sold is approximately £600,000.

"The value of each site if sold as a going concern is:

Site 1	£780,000
Site 2	£700,000
Site 3	£430,000
Site 4	£400,000
Site 5	£230,000"

Mr Carter also pointed out that the Birmingham site had been losing money for two years without a decision being taken regarding its future. Support for this site had come from sales made at the other sites.

"The Birmingham site (Site 5) used to be the leading profit maker in the company but over the last twenty years since its height of trading social and economic changes have caused a change in the local populace and local employment. The new residents in the area are not of the social-economic group that tend to buy expensive German cars."

Mr Carter asked the Board of Directors for their initial comments before arranging a two-day meeting to go into details regarding future action. He was given the following opinions.

1. The Production Director, Mr F Banks, who is in charge of the garages believes that the Birmingham site should be sold and staff laid off. In this way he believes the company can weather the recession just like many other companies are having to do, and make itself efficient ready for recovery in the economy.

2. T. Coates, the new Marketing Director appointed by George Carter, believes that they should become agents for a car that is meant for the mass market and then promote the company nationally to attract more customers. Twenty per cent of the cost of such advertising will be paid for by the German manufacturers provided their cars are mentioned in any advertising.

3. Mr Jones, the Commercial Director, believes that they should promote the garages' services locally as this would be inexpensive and the garages were currently working at half their capacity. Further, he also considers it wise to become agents for a less expensive car and also to drop their current distribution with their present German car as it ties up too much capital in each car.

4. Mr Brown, the Accounts Director, also felt that they should sell the Birmingham site to ensure liquidity for the company and then buy a small company that is in the growth area of the economy to spread their risk of investment. He also considered that their current premises could be used for other services but he wanted

to investigate the finances further before making any suggestions.

Mr Carter thanked them for their comments and informed them at the meeting that the company could raise up to £500,000 from the banks but at the cost of mortgaging their best site.

QUESTION PAPER

Wheelers Cars Ltd

TIME ALLOWED: $1\frac{1}{2}$ hours

INSTRUCTIONS

General area—Non-specific questions
Examinees may answer the three questions given below or elect to discuss other aspects of the case.

Specific questions
1. Given the financial situation of Wheelers what would be your recommendations regarding the raising of extra finances in the immediate future?
2. If Wheelers became a distributor for a car meant for the mass market how may they advertise this new appointment to potential customers?
3. In what way would you restructure Wheelers and what new services may you offer to customers of the company?

3. Procedure for answering mini-cases. In the example given in **2** above the examiners would be looking for about four or five pages of good work in the time allowed.

With mini-cases it is important at the outset to identify the main problems at the root of the situation outlined in the case history. Your work and revision practice should enable you to analyse the facts you are given adequately.

As in the example in **2** you can either answer a general question, or choose to answer more specific questions relating to the case.

(*a*) *General questions.* If you choose to answer the non-specific question:

(*i*) head each area that you intend to answer or make one statement on the area(s) of the problem that you have chosen to write on;

(*ii*) briefly analyse the situation by adopting the viewpoint of a person in the case or, preferably, put your own original interpretation of the study;

(*iii*) outline the shortcomings of the current approach or ideas given in the case and relate them to the points that you raised in (*i*) above;

(*iv*) recommend ways and provide facts, examples and sound reasoning where possible on how you would solve the problem(s). It is best to deal first with what you consider to be the major problems. Do not ignore facts or figures given in the case as they would have been put in for a good reason.

(*b*) *Specific questions.* If you choose to answer the specific questions the easiest and most reliable course to adopt, provided that you really know the subject and what you are going to write, is as follows:

(*i*) allow equal time to answering each question;

(*ii*) allow five minutes per question for arranging an essay plan;

(*iii*) write as you would in answering an analytical essay (*see* IX, **3**).

CASE STUDIES

4. Answering a case study. The approach used in answering mini-cases should be adopted in answering full case studies. However, the case to be studied is generally sent to students approximately one month before the examination so the examiner will be expecting a more detailed answer with ample use of facts and close reasoning. The best advice is to work hard on the case for that month researching, gathering facts and analysing the information given so that you are ready for the examination. One way to cover most aspects of the case is to study in groups if you can and divide the workload amongst the group members (*see* V for appropriate methods).

REPORTS

5. Reports in examinations. Generally speaking reports, theses, dissertations and projects form part of the work carried out throughout the course often requiring frequent consultation with the tutor. They therefore fall strictly beyond the scope of this book. Nevertheless, in some case study examinations students are asked to write a report on some aspect of the case.

Unless the question specifically requests you to exclude certain areas a report written under exam conditions should include the points listed in (d) to (g) below. A full report forming part of a course project would need to include all the points listed.

(a) Give the report a title.

(b) Give the reasons for the report. This can be inserted before the contents page if necessary.

(c) Include a contents page unless it is written during an examination. Include in the contents the main section headings.

(d) State your objectives in writing the report and outline your proposed method of approach.

(e) If applicable state the shortcomings of the current approach.

(f) Analyse the problem(s) first in general and then in detail giving your observations.

(g) State your recommendations for a plan of action to be effective in (i) the long-term, (ii) the medium-term, or (iii) the short-term, whichever is applicable.

(h) Where appropriate give the location and date of any interviews, meetings, etc., together with the name and position of those interviewed.

(i) Any appendixes should follow the report and should be featured in the contents list. Parts of the appendixes should be referenced in the report.

(j) Include a complete bibliography of the names and addresses of all the people interviewed (unless they are respondents to field research questionnaires).

(k) Lastly, include an index of the main topics covered.

CHECKLIST

1. If a case study or mini-case forms part of your examination work in study groups whenever possible.
2. Obtain and study any specimen reports or answers available from the examining body.

CHAPTER XII

Orals, Aurals and Practicals

"Education has for its object the formation of character."

Herbert Spencer

ORALS

1. Introduction. Oral or spoken examinations are of particular importance in certain subjects for examination such as languages and medicine, but they are also beginning to gain favour in other fields. Some of the reasons for this are as follows.

(*a*) They are more flexible than written examinations.

(*b*) The interviewer can probe deeper into a topic with the examinee.

(*c*) Some students perform better in oral than in written tests.

(*d*) Certain qualities are impossible to ascertain without an oral examination, e.g. the ability to converse freely in another language.

2. Taking an oral exam. If you feel nervous about oral examinations, you will improve your performance if you remember the following.

(*a*) They are simply an alternative to a written test so there is no need for additional fear.

(*b*) The examiner in most national examinations is not trying to trick you. His job is to try and find out how well you know and understand your subject. He or she will rarely voice approval or disapproval. Instead they will simply make comments such as "fine" or "let's move on to the next point". If a tape recorder is used it is only to ensure that you are assessed correctly. Afterwards, the examiner and another colleague may play back the conversation and agree on a grade. The point is, there is no need to be nervous.

(c) Try to avoid talking too much or too little. Politely say what you feel is necessary in answer to a question or test and say no more unless you firmly feel that your additional comment will display a deeper understanding of the topic.

(d) It is wise to read widely in your subject. Remember an oral examination is more immediate than a written one as the interviewer talks back to you. Unlike in a written examination you cannot say solely what you wish to say. If you have not adequately covered the syllabus an oral examination is more likely to reveal this than a written one.

(e) Many examinees have difficulty in settling down so loosen up a little by talking with other examinees before entering the examination room.

(f) Avoid answering too quickly. Try to maintain a normal rate of answering and take your time if you feel you need to think a little before replying.

It is worth remembering that you are subjected to a kind of oral (and aural) examination every time you are interviewed for a place at college or a job. Studying in groups will help overcome any nervousness you may have over speaking your thoughts to others and is a good method of revision (see V).

AURALS

3. Aural exams. Aural or listening examinations tend to be solely used in language tests and are closely related to oral examinations. There are, however, some aspects of which you should be aware if your performance is to be improved.

(a) If we *listen* to a conversation or story read out loud we tend to remember what was said towards the end more than what was said at the beginning because of the time delay involved. To improve your performance try to listen to conversations of a similar length to those used in the examination and concentrate on improving your recall of what was said at the beginning. Remember, in an exam you won't have an opportunity to go back over the material.

(*b*) Practise as much as possible. What you will listen to in the exam may not follow the textbooks; they will reflect the language as it is currently spoken complete with colloquialisms and idioms.

PRACTICALS

4. Introduction. Examinees often have the attitude that practicals mean simply going through the motions of a procedure. It is this attitude that causes many students not to be sufficiently analytical when undertaking practicals in lesson periods. Eventually, when faced with a question in an exam designed to assess his ability to analyse the work being performed, the examinee finds himself unable to reply satisfactorily.

5. Practical work. Whenever you have the opportunity to do practical work ensure that you carry out the following.

(*a*) Obtain as much *information* as you can on the materials and equipment you will be using, i.e. the properties of the metal, wood or plastic, and the procedures, apparatus, etc., involved.

(*b*) Develop your *ability* (*i*) to use the equipment; (*ii*) to make observations such as changes in chemicals or materials used in the test; (*iii*) to record your observations satisfactorily; (*iv*) to develop procedures or design apparatus to solve a problem.

(*c*) Learn to *analyse* what you or someone else is doing.

Before starting to do the practice required in revision, check what the emphasis is on in the examination. Is the practical designed to check your knowledge on the subject or is it more concerned with skill? As an example, an art examination is more concerned with the end result rather than the examinee's knowledge of pencils or paper. By checking up on this you will realise where you should concentrate your efforts to obtain maximum marks.

CHECKLIST

1. To improve your performance in *oral* exams practise talking as much as possible with other people—study groups are ideal for this—but in the actual exam say only what is necessary.

2. Your performance in *aural* exams can be improved in much the same way as in oral exams, but you should also practise listening to and remembering the contents of conversations of a similar length to those that will be used in the exam.

CHAPTER XIII

How the Examiners Mark Your Work

"A plausible impossibility is always preferable to an unconvincing possibility."

Aristotle

DEVISING THE QUESTIONS

1. For external exams. Examining boards generally have a *chief examiner* for each particular subject area and level who is responsible for the entire syllabus and accompanying examinations. Under the guidance of the chief examiner one or a number of *examiners* devise the actual question paper and marking schemes (*see* **4** below) which are then checked by *moderators* to ensure that it is fair, representative of the course and reflects the aims and standards of the board concerned.

The moderators also conduct random checks on the marked examination scripts to ensure that the scripts have been marked in accordance with the marking scheme and that the marking scheme is working correctly and does not contain any unforeseen bias.

2. For internal exams. The examining authority in this case will generally be your own course tutors and the examination questions will probably be set under the guidance of the department head or course tutor. These may also act as moderators at a later stage to check the suitability of the questions and the accuracy of the marking.

The intention of this chapter is to give a brief idea of how an internally set exam paper comes into being. A similar sort of procedure will be followed by external examining authorities, although, of course, the number of people involved in devising, setting, checking and marking the scripts is far greater, and the marking schemes used will vary greatly.

You are strongly advised to consult your own tutor or the relevant examining body to find out how your exam questions have been set and what criteria have been used to check them. They will generally be pleased to help you.

MARKING THE PAPERS

3. How your papers are marked. It may help you to understand how your examination papers are marked if you study the following extracts of a memo sent by one college to its tutors setting examination papers for the first time (*see* **4 to 6** below). Most examining authorities have their own procedure but this heavily abridged example may serve to illustrate the point that examining bodies do try to be fair and objective.

Students often believe that there is something bordering on mystery surrounding the marking of scripts by examiners. There is nothing further from the truth. Those responsible for setting examination papers have, like the examinees, to justify their proposals.

4. Marking schemes. Before setting the paper the tutors will be informed by the overall course tutor of the structure to be followed in that particular examination paper, i.e. two sections, three sections or no sections. A precise marking scheme must be submitted by the tutor or tutors responsible for setting the question paper. This ensures:

(*a*) that the moderator and any person marking the paper understands what answer(s) the person who set the paper was seeking;

(*b*) that the course tutor or Principal is able to check the questions for ambiguities; and possibly

(*c*) that any institute, association or inspector moderating the paper is able to make a full assessment of its accuracy and standard in relation to their requirements.

The moderators of the paper will require the tutor to adhere to a precise marking scheme for each question e.g. 20 marks with not less than a half mark being given for each correct point in the answer.

EXAMPLE

A student would be awarded 65 per cent if he or she answered the required five questions and was given the following marks out of 20 for each question:

	Marks awarded	*Moderated marks*
Q.2	18	17
Q.4	16	16
Q.5	$10\frac{1}{2}$	$10\frac{1}{2}$
Q.7	12	12
Q.9	$9\frac{1}{2}$	$9\frac{1}{2}$
TOTAL	66%	65%

Papers must be marked in the margin in red or green, with additional comments at the foot of the answer.

5. Specimen marking schemes. Each tutor is free to determine the method of marking each answer and the marks that should be awarded, but these must be detailed in writing and presented to the Registrar of Examinations (or his equivalent) when the proposed examination paper is submitted.

However, certain rules must be observed when compiling a marking scheme.

(*a*) Questions that require an "absolute answer" must be accompanied by a full answer to the question when the marking scheme is submitted. Examples of these include certain statistics, physics and mathematics questions. It must be proved that the question is capable of a correct answer in order to ensure that the question is correct in its setting.

(*b*) The major marks awarded for essay type questions should be for reasoning or analysis unless the institute or association has specifically stated that only an understanding of the principles is necessary and not an in-depth appreciation of the counter arguments that may exist concerning the application of the principles. Supporting facts will carry the next major marking element.

(*c*) For internally set mock or final examinations which set questions of an essay type students must not be asked to "list" or "note" items. The purpose of the examinations is to test powers of reasoning and retention of facts.

(d) If it is intended that examinees must answer questions from several parts of a paper that is in sections, exact instructions must be given to the examinee at the head of the examination paper.

(e) The moderator must be aware of any special material such as "log tables" that are required for answering a question.

(f) Where papers on scientific subjects involve both the theory and the application of particular principles most questions assess the student's understanding of *both* aspects.

(g) Calculators may be used in certain examinations but they must be battery operated, noiseless, non-programmable and without a print-out facility.

EXAMPLE 1

Specimen question

(a) Outline two statistical methods available for determining a sales trend.

(b) Using first linear regression plot the trend for the sales of Company X using the following figures:

Year	Sales (£000s)
1975	730
1976	790
1977	805
1978	805
1979	815
1980	826
1981	834

Suggested marking scheme for this question

Part (a)	At least four possible answers: (i) Moving averages; (ii) Cusum; (iii) 1st linear regression; and (iv) 2nd linear least squares criteria. Students should outline their value as applied.	*Marks possible*
	Each method carries 2 marks therefore:	4

Part (b)		
	Did the student recognise the type of question and the approach to adopt for its solution?	2
	Workings (including explanation)	7
	Correct graphing	5
	Correct answer and good presentation	2
	TOTAL MARKS POSSIBLE	20

In Part (*a*) the examiner could have—for a more complete marking scheme—indicated all statistical sales trend forecasting methods and outlined the value of each one.

In Part (*b*) you may notice that the content is more important than the correct answer. This is always the case in marking schemes for the following reasons.

(*a*) The student has to prove that he or she knows how to use the method. After all he could have arrived at the answer by other means such as cheating, guesswork or by mental arithmetic.

(*b*) A major part of the examination is successful communication. For example, the student may one day have to communicate knowledge of the subject to an employer who does not have a deep grasp of the principles involved.

The marking scheme for Part (*b*) therefore, should include the workings and graph that answer this question.

EXAMPLE 2

Specimen essay question

"Half the money spent on advertising is wasted." Discuss.

Suggested marking scheme for this question

General	*Marks possible*
Did the student understand that this is an absolute question that is provocative and incapable of being scientifically substantiated? Did the student recognise that it formed part of a famous speech and that it is quoted out of context?	3

Reasoning

(*a*)   Did the student recognise that there is wastage in advertising but that this should be considered against the advertising aims of various types of organisation such as:

(*i*) governments;
(*ii*) charities and trusts;
(*iii*) clubs and associations;
(*iv*) companies;
(*v*) individuals, etc.   7

(*b*)   Did the student appreciate that it may be considered that there has been no wastage if the aims were achieved, and counter this with the realisation of failed advertising and blanket advertising used to reach a small audience?   5

Concluding argument	3
"Presentation bonus"	2
TOTAL MARKS POSSIBLE	20

Note that the majority of marks were awarded for facts and analysis. It may be argued that the student should not have to recognise the speech from which the quote came and that too many marks have been given to a conclusion. This is for the tutors setting the paper to decide.

It is, of course, impossible for anyone to write a definitive answer to a question that contains such scope for many value judgments. Reasonably precise indicators are what is required in the marking scheme for such a question.

The "Presentation bonus" is for originality, logical presentation, layout, and neat and legible work. However, if the tutor considers that this separate heading is not necessary he or she may absorb the marks for this element into the other headings of the marking scheme for this particular question.

OUTSIDE THE MARKING SCHEME

6. Essays not covered by the marking scheme. It may be found that when the answers are analysed a student has presented an excellent answer that is not in accord with the marking scheme.

If many students did this then it is probable that the tutor did not consider the marking scheme deeply enough, or that the students have been given the wrong information during their lectures. If, however, it is just one student then it may be that he or she has seen the problem from an unusual but valid viewpoint.

In either case, the problem must be brought to the attention of the Principal via the course tutor or Registrar to ensure that the student or students are not penalised in any way and, if necessary, the moderators are informed.

7. Conclusion. In short there is no magical formula for obtaining a pass; it is simply a matter of making sure you reach the standards required by your course and the examiners.

Remember, not all exams are tests of perfect English! The important aspect is that you make yourself clearly understood in your answer.

CHECKLIST

1. Find out from your course tutor (if it is an internal exam) or the examining body (if it is an external exam) what procedure will be followed in setting the exam questions.
2. Find out if you can what sort of marking scheme will be used in your exam.
3. If you have problems in answering a question during the exam for which you are sure you have done sufficient work consult your tutor.

CHAPTER XIV

Common Failings

"The one real object of education is to leave a man in the condition of continually asking questions."
Bishop Creighton

WRITTEN EXAMINATIONS

1. False assumptions. A written exam requires you to present your knowledge in a logical fashion in response to a particular question set at a particular level and completed within a restricted time. As we have seen, to be able to do this requires a certain amount of preparation; however, the general attitude of many students to this preparation seems to be a guarantee for failure. Consider the following assumptions.

"I'm not worried about practising and mock examinations as *I'll do well on the day.*"

"I know the subject well and the examiner will recognise this, and therefore he will pass me."

"I passed the *mock* exams well so I will pass the finals."

"It doesn't matter if I do not write much and as long as what I write is correct the examiner will pass me."

"Writing the language well in which the examination is set is not important provided I write the right things."

"It doesn't matter about going to all the lessons as long as I go in the month preceding the examination and do the revision."

All of these assumptions are false, and just to prove the point the following paragraphs examine each in turn. The observations are based on experience in setting examinations and reading the examiner's reports of examining authorities.

2. "I'll do well on the day." This attitude is usually adopted by what could be termed "sloppy" students. They are sloppy in their academic careers and often carry this attitude into their working careers being unable to do satisfactory reports on time for their employers.

Quite often this attitude is held by students taking internal examinations in the belief that closer to the examinations the lecturer will subtly indicate what questions will be asked. When this doesn't happen they suddenly panic and as the examinations are so close they cannot study effectively with the result that they usually fail. If they pass they are aware that it was more by luck than management and are therefore less pleased with their achievement.

3. "I know the subject well." A student with this type of attitude usually writes all he or she knows about a topic irrespective of what the question is asking. Let us make this clear. The examiner is not interested in *how much* knowledge you have on the subject. He is trying to discover if you can *apply* that knowledge by selecting relevant parts in order to answer the problems that he has set. Indeed, the question may be more concerned with your ability to analyse the problem than whether you can remember a large amount of facts or apply them in finding a solution.

4. "I passed the mock exams." "Mock" exams are rarely set at the level required by the final examination. They are usually set half way through the course as an indicator of your progression *up to that point*. If you pass the mocks but do not continue to progress at the same rate up to the final examinations you have no foundation for assuming that you can pass the actual examinations.

5. "It doesn't matter if I do not write much." Examination questions are designed to test the outstanding student as well as the poor and average candidate. Thus the question will also allow enough scope for relatively deep and lengthy analysis in the time available.

Generally speaking, unless the question simply requests "listing" or "brief notes", students should aim to cover at least two to three sides of A4 sized paper (depending on the size and neatness of their handwriting) if they are to do justice to a question where approximately thirty-eight minutes can be allowed for writing the essay.

Be careful, however, not to go for length to the detriment of content. There is a balance, so consult your tutor if necessary.

6. "Writing the language well is not important." Writing the right things in your answer and being able to interpret the questions correctly *does* rely on your command of the language in which the examination is set. Although examiners are not looking for a perfect command of the language—particularly in non-language examinations—they do expect you to be able to use the language well enough to be able to present your argument effectively. This is particularly the case where good use of language may be important in your eventual career, e.g. as an accountant or barrister.

Throughout your course and revision it is wise to try to improve your use of the language at every opportunity. Do not ignore the study of the language simply because you do not like this subject.

7. "It doesn't matter about going to all the lessons." Students with this type of attitude are like those in **2** above. They panic near exam time and shortly after the examinations are unable to recall what they have learned because they did not learn it over a long enough period. They have wasted their revision period catching up on what they should have learned during their course instead of using it to review what they already know. In the examination they find that they are unable to write essays in sufficient detail because they do not know enough about the subject.

8. Some final advice. *Do all the work your tutor considers necessary to obtain a good pass.* Bear in mind that examiners do like originality, but don't be different for the sake of it. One way to ensure that you can write effectively and with confidence is to read widely on your subject so that you are not simply regurgitating in the exam what you were taught by your tutor.

CASE STUDIES

9. Failings in case studies. It doesn't matter what the case study is concerned with, whether it be the modernising of an African village, launching a new product or feeding an army, the same principles apply in answering the questions and so the same type of faults will be found. The major ones are as follows.

(*a*) Students cannot write and present a report correctly. Reports are not always required, but when they are students often answer as though they had been asked for an essay.

(*b*) Many students appear to have formulated their attitude towards the case in advance. Therefore they do not answer the question asked but the question that they would *like* to answer.

(*c*) Many students do not answer the questions in a logical sequence to give a cumulative and integrated overall answer.

(*d*) Examinees make all their notes relating to the case before the examination with their tutor, and so do not effectively analyse the case themselves or develop their own opinion. The results are that, if they are asked questions which were not adequately covered by the tutor, they cannot use their minds quickly enough in the examination to provide an effective answer, and when they are given questions that they can answer each examinee answers in the same way thus showing no originality. Remember, YOU are being examined, not your tutor.

(*e*) Examinees ignore time scales. They do not appear to fully understand short, medium and long-term in relation to the particular case.

(*f*) Many examinees do not appear to have practised writing against case studies under mock examination conditions. They write too much on one aspect of the paper and too little on another.

(*g*) Examinees do not fully understand the balance between *quantitative* and *qualitative* considerations. Often they suggest, for example, re-organising a company or moving people around on a housing estate without regard to the likely effect in human terms of such a move. Likewise, examinees often suggest changes in company policy or additions to factory machinery without any regard to the costs, necessary changes in budget or whether the community, organisation or government can afford such measures.

THE EXAMINER'S POINT OF VIEW

10. Keeping the examiner happy. Students frequently irritate the examiner marking their scripts in a number of ways that could easily be avoided. Examiners are only human after all—although they do try to be impartial—so try to avoid the following niggling habits that could count against you when your paper is being marked.

1. *Illegible handwriting.* This is probably the most frequent complaint by examiners. Look at the following examples:
   Only the third example is really legible. It is worth remembering that external examiners are usually paid a set amount for each script that they mark regardless of the

During this time dangers had taken...

Pictures in galleries form a mackcloth of beauty...

Answers to such questions are only possible...

   amount of time it takes. It is a trying test of their patience to present them with handwriting that takes five times longer than normal to decipher.
2. *Writing in the margin.* The margin is *solely* for the examiner to make comments in—students frequently use it for rough workings.
3. *Rough workings.* Always show your workings so that the examiner may award marks for knowing how to arrive at the correct answer. If you do not show your workings you are losing marks needlessly.
4. *Additional papers.* Make sure that any additional papers that you use in the exam are put in the right order when you attach them to the answer book. If they are in the wrong order it wastes the examiner's time and creates a bad impression.
5. *Incorrect numbering.* Make sure that you have put the correct number to each of the questions that you have answered at the beginning of each answer you give and—where requested—on or inside the front cover of the answer book.
6. *Appealing to the examiner.* Do not write personal notes to the examiner at the end of your essays giving excuses as to why you did not do better. They will have no effect on the examiner

and may bias his judgment against you. Similarly avoid appealing to the examiner in the first person as you write your essays.

7. *Drawings and diagrams.* Avoid using fountain pens when drawing diagrams as the ink is liable to smudge before the examiner sees it. Always use, if you can, a ruler, compass, etc., when drawing your diagrams as it creates a much neater impression.

8. *Half-finished sentences.* Make sure that you finish your essays in time to avoid leaving a half-finished sentence. You should pace yourself correctly.

CHECKLIST

1. Do not make assumptions about the way you will perform on the actual day of the examination. Only by practising your essay technique and having learned the necessary information can you be sure of passing.

2. Try to be original if you can, but do not be so simply for the sake of appearing clever. The examiners will see through this and may penalise you if you stray from the point.

3. If you are writing a case study report present it in the correct manner. Avoid merely repeating what you have been told by your tutor.

4. Try not to irritate the examiner unnecessarily. Clear handwriting, keeping out of the margins and the correct numbering of questions answered are a few of the ways you can avoid creating a bad impression.

CHAPTER XV

General Preparation for the Exam

"You can't think rationally on an empty stomach."
Lord Reith

PHYSICAL PREPARATION

1. Health and exercise. If a runner is to be successful in his sport he has to:

—exercise;
—practise;
—study the tactics of the sport;
—have the correct equipment;
—have the right mental attitude;
—eat properly;
—obtain adequate rest and relaxation.

It is unlikely that anyone would argue with these points, and yet when it comes to examinations many people believe that you only need intelligence to pass. Intelligence is of little value if you do not have the knowledge and knowledge is of no value if it cannot be expressed *when required*.

Approaching the time of the examination you should be mentally calm and physically healthy. Assuming that you have only four weeks left until the examinations let us look at some dos and don'ts with regard to your health and mental well being.

(*a*) Don't start on a diet. This is not the time to be distracted with the thought of food.

(*b*) Don't start eating food with a low nutritional value. Try to maintain a healthy natural diet and avoid eating heavy starchy foods such as large desserts. These will only make you feel sluggish.

(*c*) Don't drink too much coffee and tea as they contain substances which excite rather than calm your nerves. Try drinking chocolate or, better still, fresh fruit juices or water. Both are available from reputable chain stores.

(*d*) If you were thinking of stopping smoking don't try now. However, do practise not smoking between 9 a.m. to 1 p.m. and 2 p.m. to 5 p.m. as these are generally the examination times when you will not be allowed to smoke.

Full-time students usually do not have problems in this respect as they are not allowed to smoke in classes anyway, but correspondence students do and often make excuses to visit the toilet during the examination in order to smoke. This is a waste of valuable time.

(*e*) Do increase the roughage in your diet so that your bodily functions are kept in good order. Again proprietary stores usually have tasty bran cereals to meet this requirement.

(*f*) Don't spend all your time revising. Get plenty of fresh air and exercise and indulge in some relaxing pursuit.

(*g*) If you live with your family remind them that this is not the time to present you with problems that can wait until after the examinations.

If you develop a cold during the examinations ask your doctor to prescribe medicine to keep you breathing freely, stop your eyes running and prevent any possible headache. Many people do not like to take such medicines, but remember you may have to wait another six to nine months for the next set of examinations.

BEFORE THE EXAMINATION

2. Checklist for the day before.
1. Unwind mentally. Do not do any studying except to clear up one or two points with your tutor.
2. If you are having a drink to celebrate the end of term, stop early and well before you begin to feel the effects of the alcohol.

3. Get plenty of fresh air because you will probably be in a stuffy hall the whole of the next day.
4. Re-check that you have got the time and directions to the examination correct. Have the clothes ready that you will wear the next day.

"It's too late to worry about that now!"

5. Check that you have any identity document that may be required by the invigilators and, of course, your candidate number.
6. Check that you have the equipment required for the examination. Where possible take two of each, including calculator batteries if a calculator can be used. (Remember, even where calculators can be used they normally must be battery operated, noiseless and without a print-out facility.)
7. Do something relaxing in the evening and then go to bed early ready for an early start to the next day.

ON THE EXAMINATION DAY

3. Checklist for the day.
1. Put on clean warm clothes and, if it is a cool day, take an extra

102

jumper with you in case you feel cold during the examination. Examination halls are generally colder and more draughty around feet or leg height. Dress to allow for this situation.
2. Eat a good breakfast, but don't drink too much. In this way you will not feel hungry during the examination.

"But all I said was the exam starts in one minute."

3. Try to arrive at the examination hall half an hour before the start to allow for any delays in transport and give yourself time to relax.
4. Do not enter into a conversation with other examinees; they will just confuse you and start you questioning your own knowledge on the subject at a time when you need to feel reasonably confident. Look out of the window instead; you may not see a nice view for some time.
5. If you can, visit the toilet just before you enter the examination hall.
6. If you smoke, it may be wise to take some sweets to suck into the examination if, of course, the invigilators let you.

CHECKLIST

1. Aim to be physically fit and mentally alert as you approach your exam period. Make sure you eat nutritious food and avoid too many artificial stimulants such as coffee and tea or excessive amounts of alcohol. If you smoke, make sure you can do without a cigarette for the duration of the exam. Get plenty of fresh air and exercise.
2. On the day before, relax. Check details such as the time and place of the exam. Gather together any equipment you need. Go to bed early.
3. On the day itself, dress appropriately. Have a good breakfast. Aim to arrive early so that you can relax before the exam begins.
4. Do your best! That's all anyone expects of you.

Students' Queries:
Before the Exam

Q: I become very nervous nearing examinations. Do you think I should take a sedative before going into the examination hall?

A: No, is the short answer. It could be argued that candidates should be slightly anxious about the examination as it mentally prepares them for work. It is only "panic" that you are trying to avoid. Don't dull or over excite your system with drugs, alcohol or excessive amounts of coffee or tea.

Q: Do you have any special advice for students following a home study course?

A: Two of the main problems with home study students are:
   (i) they do not read extensively; and
   (ii) they have not had the experience of a mock exam to let them know how they would perform under exam conditions.
   Therefore, read more than just the manuals sent to you. Most home study manuals are very good but a few lack sufficient coverage of the subject to give the student the thorough grounding necessary for the exams. Also, set yourself mock exams as described in VI.

Q: What can I do if I have a problem with my health which prevents me from attending an examination?

A: Consult the examining authority. Many have a procedure for examining candidates who are likely to be unable to attend the next few sessions due to continuing health problems.

Q: What happens if I'm in a wheelchair? Can I take the exams?

A: The invigilators are prepared for this but you must inform the examining authority first and you may possibly have to make your own way to the exam and your place in the exam hall or have other special arrangements made.

Q: What if I or one of my family have an accident on the day of the examination? Will any allowance or arrangement be made?

A: Few examining authorities can help in such circumstances as they would be inundated with bogus appeals. If it is an internally examined course arrangements may be possible. Consult your course tutor.

Q: Living on my own, I often find at revision time that a lot of my time is spent doing household chores and cooking. What do you suggest?

A: Eat at the college or an inexpensive restaurant. If your parents live near and you have a good relationship move home for the revision period. Don't be too fussy about cleaning. If it can wait let it wait. You may be well advised to supplement your diet with daily multi-vitamin tablets.

Q: If it is possible, do you think it is wise to take a holiday during the revision period?

A: Yes, as long as you don't mind failing. The only justification for a holiday is when a student is working and taking a part-time day or evening course and intends to have a week or two off from his employment to revise well because he/she has not had sufficient opportunity during the course. Other holidays are usually distracting and inappropriate at revision time.

Q: What should I do if I know that malpractice regarding the examination has taken place before the examination?

A: Inform your tutor immediately and ensure that you obtain a final decision with regard to his course of action. This should include informing the examining authority if you have facts in support of your accusations.

CHAPTER XVI

The Examination and After

"I had a good education but it never went to my head."

Alan Bennett

DURING THE EXAMINATION

1. Checklist and Review.

1. Read the instructions relating to the examination very carefully.
2. Spend five minutes considering all the questions on the examination paper before attempting to answer any.
3. Give a star rating to the questions that you believe that you can confidently answer and start with the one(s) which you have awarded the most stars.
4. Circle the *key words* in the questions which clearly define what is being required and keep them in mind as you write the essay plan and essay.
5. Allow a few minutes before starting each answer to give thought to the question and to write an essay plan sketching out your proposed answer. Always refer back to what the question is asking as you write each note that will constitute a paragraph in your essay.
6. Don't forget to cross through your notes when they are completed and start the answer on a new page.
7. Don't write all that you know about a subject irrespective of what is being asked. This may lose you marks as the examiner will believe you are not able to concentrate your mind on *what was asked*.
8. Try to write in an easy and free flowing style. Avoid

continually repeating certain words or starting sentences with the same words, e.g. "therefore" or "consequently", or ending an essay with "finally . . ." or "in conclusion . . .".

9. Refer to your watch every now and again to make certain that you are on target for answering all the questions required.

10. Remember there are no golden rules as to the length of an essay, but in general two to three pages of A4 are needed to present a complete answer, particularly in answering an analytical question, though this will depend on the size of your handwriting.

11. Do not re-write the question before you start to answer. The marker knows the question; he wants the answer.

12. Try to write as legibly as possible.

13. Use all the time available in the examination. By doing so you will probably produce more useful work for examining. If you do finish before time read what you have done and make additions or amendments as required. Pace yourself to avoid finishing too early.

14. Do not write in the margins; these are for the marker to use.

15. If the examination question requires an essay as an answer, do not present any headings or lines in other colours such as red or green. This is wasting time and does not gain marks.

16. DON'T CHEAT. You are likely to be barred for life from taking any further examinations with that board. It simply isn't worth it.

17. If anyone talks to you do not talk back. Raise your hand and direct the invigilator to the other person. You may be accused of cheating when you were simply lending a ruler.

18. If you have not been allocated a seat obtain one near natural light, but avoid sitting close to radiators as they may make you drowsy.

19. Put your watch on the table to help you pace your work. Set it in agreement with the examination clock in the room or hall.

20. If your memory fails you try to start a thought process by thinking of first principles. If that fails, relax, stare into space and it may drift back to you. If not, start another piece of work and return later. Don't spend time dwelling too long on the problem and possibly working yourself into a panic.

21. If you remember nothing else keep the following in mind:

PLAN   Read the paper carefully. Give a star rating to the question that you prefer to answer. Underline the key points and prepare an essay plan.

PANIC   If you feel yourself becoming agitated stop, relax and look at anything except the paper until you feel calm again.

PRESENTATION   Set out your work in a neat, legible and logical way.

PACING   Do an even amount of work on each question in the time allowed.

STOP   Carry on working until time is called. If you finish before the end, re-read your work and improve it where possible closing off each piece of work only when you are completely satisfied.

2. After the examination. If you have an examination in the afternoon, follow the procedure as already outlined. Otherwise go home and relax, doing nothing more than preparing yourself for your next examination. Above all else do not dwell on the examination that you have just taken.

MISCONDUCT

3. Informing the examining body. If you believe that you have seen things in the examination that should be brought to the attention of the examining body, then make sure that they are fundamental to the good conduct of the examination. These would include the following.

(*a*) Questions have been set that were not in keeping with the syllabus. Discuss this first with your subject tutors.

(*b*) A considerable number of students have been cheating. This is usually more important where:

    (*i*) examination papers were obtained prior to the examination;

    (*ii*) gross negligence was shown on behalf of the invigilators.

In all cases make sure that you have the facts in the right perspective by discussing the events with other students and your tutor.

Do not feel embarrassed about informing the examining body. They prefer to hear from staff or students so that they can take action rather than receive bad publicity. No reputable body ever wishes to be associated with malpractice.

4. Appeals against decisions. If you believe that you have been unfairly marked, check to see if the examining body operates an appeals procedure and act in accordance with their instructions. If one does not exist, do not assume that the examining body is inefficient or is unreasonable. It may be that they are extremely cautious and check and regulate all markings and moderations before issuing results.

Make certain that you have facts to substantiate your claim before you approach the examining board. In any event talk it over with your tutor.

CHECKLIST

1. During the exam try to put into practice the advice given throughout this book. The checklist given in 1 above will help you.
2. After the exam try not to dwell on the exam you have just taken. Prepare yourself for the next exam or simply go home and relax.
3. If you feel you have a grievance—either there was some form of misconduct during the exam or you later feel you have been unfairly marked—discuss the matter with your tutor and fellow students before informing the examining body. Take this last step only if you are certain there is something they should be aware of.

Students' Queries:
During the Exam

Q: What should I do if I discover, when re-reading my work, that I have misinterpreted a question and thus written a completely wrong answer?

A: Write a brief note underneath your answer explaining that you realise what you have done, and quickly note down how you would have answered now that you realise your mistake.

Do as you are consistently told by tutors:

(i) don't underline your answer as you may wish to make additions later;

(ii) allow yourself enough time at the end of the examination to glance quickly over what you did.

Q: Is the person marking my examination script the final judge of whether I pass or fail?

A: Definitely not, unless the examining body is completely inefficient at setting examinations. One or several additional people will have checked the paper and marking scheme when it was set as well as a random selection of scripts when they are completed.

Without going into too much detail, the paper, marking scheme and completed scripts will, at least, be moderated by another tutor in the same subject. At most there could be Moderators, Regulators, Chief Examiners, Chief Assessors, Examination Committees, Appeals Committees and even a computer involved in ensuring that the examination was fairly set and marked to the required standard.

Q: What would happen if I was stupid enough to cheat and got caught?

A: The least that would happen is that the paper would not be marked, and at most you would be thrown off the course for good and barred from taking any other examinations with that particular examining body. It is really NOT WORTH IT!

Q: How many times can one re-sit an examination?

A: Don't think in these terms. Some external examining authorities do not permit more than two sittings. On failing the two sittings the student would not be allowed to complete the course.

ON A PERSONAL NOTE

If you have read the whole of this book you shouldn't have any trouble with your next examination, but just to cover every eventuality:

GOOD LUCK!

APPENDIX

M & E Handbooks for Revision

M & E Handbooks are established as recommended reading for examination syllabuses all over the world. Because each Handbook covers its subject comprehensively but concisely, books in the series form a vital part of many university, college, school and home study courses. Each Handbook includes numerous self-testing questions at the end of each chapter, text-referenced for easy checking, and an appendix which advises on examination technique. For these reasons Handbooks are also ideal for pre-examination revision. Regularly updated and competitively priced, Handbooks are therefore the perfect choice for anyone who wants to grasp the essentials of a subject quickly and thoroughly.

Advanced Economics
G.L. Thirkettle
0164 0   2nd edition

"A" Level Law
Barry Jones
0160 8   1st edition

"A" Level Physics
M. Chapple
Vol. 1—Mechanics and Heat
0154 3   2nd edition
Vol. 2—Wave Motion:
Light and Sound
0155 1   2nd edition
Vol. 3—Electricity and Modern
Physics
0158 6   2nd edition

Applied Economics
Edmund Seddon & J.D.S.
Appleton
0177 2   3rd edition

Applied Mathematics
H.J. Vincent
0137 3   1st edition

Auditing
Leslie R. Howard
0178 0   7th edition
ELBS edition available

Bankruptcy Law
P.W.D. Redmond, revised by
I.M. McCallum
0264 7   7th edition

Basic Accounting
J.O. Magee
0284 1   2nd edition

Basic Book-keeping
J.O. Magee
0274 4   2nd edition

Basic Botany
Claire Skellern & Paul Rogers
0255 8   1st edition

Basic Economics
G.L. Thirkettle
0298 1   5th edition

Basic French
Arnold Kellett
0250 7   1st edition

Basic Law
L.B. Curzon
0245 0   1st edition
Basic Mathematics
W.M. Harper & L.W.T. Stafford
0287 6   1st edition
Basic Sociology
F.J. Wright & F. Randall
0291 4   4th edition
Biology—Advanced Level
P.T. Marshall
0268 X   3rd edition
British Government and Politics
F. Randall
2407 1   3rd edition
British Political History 1784–1939
S.T. Miller
0256 6   1st edition
British Social Services
F. Randall
0286 8   3rd edition
Business Administration
L. Hall
0269 8   3rd edition
ELBS edition available
Business and Financial Management
B.K.R. Watts
0289 2   4th edition
Business Mathematics
L.W.T. Stafford
0282 5   2nd edition
ELBS edition available
Business Organisation
Ronald R. Pitfield
0295 7   2nd edition
ELBS edition available
Business Systems
R.G. Anderson
0254 X   1st edition
ELBS edition available
Business Typewriting
Sylvia F. Parks
0294 9   3rd edition

Capital Gains Tax
Vera di Palma
0460 7   5th edition
Capital Transfer Tax
R.C. Ind
0392 9   2nd edition
Cases in Banking Law
Philip A. Gheerbrant, revised by David Palfreman
0477 1   3rd edition
Cases in Company Law
M.C. Oliver
0466 6   3rd edition
Cases in Consumer Law
G.H. Samuel
0377 5   1st edition
Cases in Contract Law
W.T. Major
0480 1   3rd edition
Cases in Criminal Law
L.B. Curzon
0376 7   2nd edition
Cases in Income Tax Law
Henry Toch
0378 3   1st edition
Cases in Tort
L.A.J. Armour & G.H. Samuel
0356 2   1st edition
Case Studies in Auditing
J. Santocki
0373 2   2nd edition
Case Studies in Systems Design
R.G. Anderson
0387 2   1st edition
Catering: Food and Drink
E.J. Hilton
0352 X   1st edition
Chemistry for "O" Level
George Usher
1528 5   1st edition
College Physics
E. Gillam & R.M. King
Volume 1
0326 0   1st edition
ELBS edition available

Volume 2
0327 9   1st edition
ELBS edition available
Commercial and Industrial Law
Anne R. Ruff
0464 X   2nd edition
Company Accounts
J.O. Magee
0470 4   3rd edition
Company Law
M.C. Oliver
0475 5   9th edition
Company Secretarial Practice
L. Hall, revised by G.M. Thom
0478 X   6th edition
Computer Science
J.K. Atkin
0396 1   2nd edition
Constitutional and Administrative Law
I.N. Stevens
0398 8   1st edition
Consumer Credit
R.G. Lawson
0399 6   1st edition
Consumer Law
M.J. Leder
0393 7   1st edition
Conveyancing Law
P.H. Kenny & C. Bevan
0482 8   2nd edition
Corporation Tax
B.S. Topple
0467 4   5th edition
Cost Accounting
—*see* Cost and Management Accounting Volume 1
Cost and Management Accounting
W.M. Harper
Vol. 1 Cost Accounting
0468 2   1st edition
Vol. II Management Accounting
0469 0   1st edition
ELBS edition available

Criminal Law
L.B. Curzon
0481 X   4th edition
Data Processing and Management Information Systems
R.G. Anderson
0431 3   4th edition
Economic Geography
H. Robinson
0577 8   3rd edition
An Economic History of England
D.J. Chappell
0587 5   1st edition
Economics for "O" Level
L.B. Curzon
0595 6   4th edition
Economics for Professional Studies
Henry Toch
0568 9   2nd edition
Elements of Banking
D.P. Whiting
0585 9   2nd edition
Elements of Commerce
Charles O'Connor
0586 7   3rd edition
Elements of Finance for Managers
B.K.R. Watts
0551 4   1st edition
Elements of Insurance
D.S. Hansell
0563 8   3rd edition
English Legal History
L.B. Curzon
0578 6   2nd edition
English Legal System
J.P. Price
0547 6   1st edition
English for Professional Examinations
J.R.L. McIntyre
0559 X   2nd edition

Equity
L.B. Curzon
0567 0   3rd edition
European History 1789–1914
C.A. Leeds
0575 1   2nd edition
Europe Since the Second World War
J.R. Thackrah
0576 X   1st edition
Family Law
P.J. Pace
0647 2   2nd edition
Finance of Foreign Trade
D.P. Whiting
0638 3   5th edition
French for Science Students
Arnold Kellett
0624 3   1st edition
General Principles of English Law
P.W.D. Redmond, revised by J.P. Price & I.N. Stevens
0725 8   5th edition
Geology
A.W.R. Potter & H. Robinson
0742 8   2nd edition
ELBS edition available
Human Geography
H. Robinson
0813 0   3rd edition
Human Resources Management
H.T. Graham
0822 X   4th edition
Human and Social Biology
George Usher
0808 4   1st edition
Income Tax 1983/84
Henry Toch
0970 6   13th edition
Industrial Administration
J.C. Denyer, revised by J. Batty
0953 6   3rd edition
Industrial Management Services

H. Beeley
0942 0   2nd Edition
Intermediate Accounts
L.W.J. Owler
0936 6   3rd edition
International Marketing
L.S. Walsh
0968 4   2nd edition
Introduction to Ecology
J.C. Emberlin
0965 X   1st edition
Introduction to Office Practice
(Previously known as *Clerical Duties*)
J.C. Denyer, revised by A.L. Mugridge
0483 6   4th edition
Jurisprudence
L.B. Curzon
1000 3   1st edition
Labour Economics
J.D.S. Appleton
2703 8   3rd edition
Labour Law
M. Wright
1257 X   3rd edition
Land Law
L.B. Curzon
1259 6   4th edition
Landlord and Tenant
J.M. Male
1251 0   1st edition
Land Surveying
Ramsay J.P. Wilson
2705 4   3rd edition
Law of Banking
David Palfreman
1258 8   2nd edition
Law of Contract
W.T. Major
2707 0   6th edition
Law of Evidence
L.B. Curzon
1244 8   1st edition

Law of Succession
L.B. Curzon
1256 1   2nd edition

Law of Torts
J.G.M. Tyas
2704 6   4th edition

Law of Trusts
L.B. Curzon
1255 3   2nd edition

Management Accounting
–*see* Cost and Management
Accounting Volume II

Management, Planning and Control
R.G. Anderson
1277 4   1st edition

Marketing
G.B. Giles
2804 2   4th edition
ELBS edition available

Marketing Research
Tony Proctor & Marilyn A. Stone
1291 X   1st edition

Mathematics for Economists
L.W.T. Stafford
1296 0   2nd edition
ELPS edition available

Meetings
L. Hall
1299 5   2nd edition

Mercantile Law
P.W.D. Redmond, revised by
R.G. Lawson
1288 X   5th edition

Microcomputing
R.G. Anderson
2805 0   2nd edition

Modern Commercial Knowledge
L.W.T. Stafford
1399 1   4th edition

Modern Economic History
Edmund Seddon
1286 3   3rd edition

Modern Marketing
Frank Jefkins
2802 6   1st edition

Modern Mathematics
G. Nunn
1391 6   1st edition

Office Administration
J.C. Denyer, revised by
A.L. Mugridge
1540 4   4th edition

"O" Level Physics
M. Chapple
1531 5   2nd edition

Operational Research
W.M. Harper & H.C. Lim
1539 0   2nd edition
ELBS edition available

Organic Chemistry
W. Templeton
1537 4   1st edition
ELBS edition available

Organisation and Methods
R.G. Anderson
1536 6   2nd edition

An Outline of Monetary Theory
J.L. Hanson
1533 1   4th edition

Partnership Accounts
J.O. Magee
1666 4   2nd edition
ELBS edition available

Partnership Law
P.W.D. Redmond
1674 5   11th edition

Physical Geography
H. Robinson
1670 2   2nd edition

Political Studies
C.A. Leeds
1694 X   3rd edition

Practice of Banking
E.P. Doyle, revised by J.E. Kelly
1755 5   3rd edition

Principles of Accounts
E.F. Castle & N.P. Owens
1692 3   6th edition

**Private International Law:
Conflict of Laws**
A.W. Scott
1684 2   2nd edition

Production Management
H.A. Harding
1688 5   3rd edition

Public Administration
Michael P. Barber, revised by
Roger Stacey
1754 7   3rd edition

Public Relations
Frank Jefkins
1764 4   2nd edition

Purchasing
C.K. Lysons
1752 0   1st edition

Quantitative Geography
R.G. Woodcock & M.J. Bailey
1703 2   1st edition

Retailing
Roger Cox
1860 8   1st edition

Roman Law
L.B. Curzon
1853 5   1st edition

Sale of Goods
W.T. Major
1966 3   4th edition

Sales and Sales Management
P. Allen
1962 0   2nd edition

**Secretarial and Administra-
tive Practice**
L. Hall
1968 X   4th edition

**Society and The State
1750–1950**
S.T. Miller
1963 9   1st edition

Statistics
W.M. Harper
1988 4   4th edition

Stores Management
R.J. Carter
1979 5   1st edition

**Town and Country Planning
Law**
A.M. Williams
2031 9   1st edition

**Twentieth-Century History
1900–45**
C.A. Leeds
2025 4   1st edition

Index